Survival Japanese

How to Communicate
without Fuss or Fear
Instantly

Boye De Mente is an acknowledged authority on
the Orient and the author of more than 30 books.
Survival Japanese is his sixth in the Japan Quick-
Guide series. He first came to Japan in 1949 with
the U.S. Army Security Agency and has been
involved with Japan as a journalist, editor,
lecturer, and writer ever since.

Survival Japanese

How to Communicate without Fuss or Fear Instantly

by

Boye Lafayette De Mente

YENBOOKS

YENBOOKS are published and distributed
by the Charles E. Tuttle Company, Inc.
of Rutland, Vermont & Tokyo, Japan
with editorial offices at
2-6 Suido 1-chome, Bunkyo-ku, Tokyo 112

LCC Card No. 91-67636
ISBN 0-8048-1681-6

First printing, 1992
Third printing, 1998

Printed in Singapore

Contents

Contents

Contents

Overcoming Instant Illiteracy

Hundreds of thousands of people who arrive in Japan each year go through an experience that is the equivalent of suddenly being struck deaf and dumb. They go from being literate—even brilliant—in their own culture to not being able to speak, understand, read, or write the language of their host country, and to being equally ignorant of the nonverbal language of Japan as well.

If this situation continues for any length of time, the experience results in a trauma known as culture shock—which in extreme cases can cause serious mental and physical damage; sometimes even death.

Short-time visitors to Japan are not likely to suffer significant health problems because of their sudden inability to interact with the culture surrounding them. But there is perhaps no more frustrating feeling than not being able to communicate with other people when we want to or need to. Where visiting business-men are concerned, the handicap of not being able to communicate directly with their Japanese counterparts, even on the most basic level, has far more serious implications.

At a recent dinner in Tokyo with the president of an American company and his Japanese guests, the frustration of the foreign visitor was evident for all to see. Finally, he said in utter exasperation: "God! If I only knew *survival* Japanese!" That is what this book is all about.

Most people use fewer than 1,000 words of their own native language in going about their daily affairs. It is not so much how many words one knows but what those words are and how they are used. This is particularly true in the case of a second, foreign language. With a vocabulary of only 300 Japanese words you can communicate several thousand ideas— not only enough to survive but also to enjoy yourself at the same time.

Many Americans in particular seem to have a foreign language phobia. Some have extreme difficulty in pronouncing a single foreign word correctly. This fear might be the result of cultural conditioning stemming from a deep-rooted feeling that speaking a foreign language is un-American; that it is a black mark that cannot be erased.

Most Americans are now intellectually sophisticated enough to know this fear of foreign languages is invalid, and to recognize the social as well as economic benefits of being multi-lingual and multi-cultural. But they are still handicapped by the emotional residue of generations of trying to get away from any hint of foreignness.

Survival Japanese is designed to help break this emotional barrier by phoneticizing, in English, every word and phrase in the book. Besides helping to suppress the emotional reaction to the language, the phonetics make it possible for the user to begin communicating immediately, greatly reducing the trauma of cross-cultural illiteracy. I am indebted to my daughter, Demetra De Mente, for suggestions that greatly improved this book.

How to Use This Book

Despite the forbidding appearance of Japanese when it is written in the Chinese ideograms known as *Kanji* (Kahn-jee) or "Chinese characters," the language is made up of precise syllables that are in fact quite easy to pronounce (people who are not familiar with the language confuse the difficulty of getting several words out in a smooth flow with a phonetic complexity that does not exist).

Unlike Chinese, Japanese is pronounced in a straight-forward manner without complicating tones. The only variations in Japanese are double consonants and double vowels that require a slight change in pronunciation. The grammatical structure of Japanese differs from Chinese as well as English, but that does not make it more difficult to learn. Looking at the order of the subject, verb, and object in a Japanese sentence, saying it is "backward" and complaining that it doesn't make sense is foolish. Of course it makes sense.

Japanese is a very flexible language. You can switch the order of words and phrases around to a surprising degree, even leave things out and it not only makes sense but is acceptable in ordinary conversation. This can be a problem to those who want everything to follow one precise rule and regard this characteristic of the language as a serious complication. But looked at another way, it makes the language *easier* to use.

There are three distinct levels of Japanese that might be called formal, standard and vulgar. These levels are different enough that they are practically dialects within themselves. It is in fact very difficult to become fluent in each of these levels. It is almost like learning separate languages. But being able to communicate effectively in standard Japanese is enough for the average foreigner to at least build a foot-bridge across the language gap.

Survival Japanese is standard Japanese. I make only a few references to grammar. In the early stages of any language study it often serves only to complicate things. The secret to language learning is to mimic the way native speakers use it, without any thought of its structure. After a while the grammar becomes imprinted on your mind, and making up correctly structured sentences becomes automatic.

This learning process is based on nothing more

mysterious than repeating the words and sentences *out loud,* always out loud—a process that imprints the sound on the ear and memory, and just as important if not more so, trains the mouth and tongue to mechanically produce the necessary syllables in a smooth flow. One of the prime reasons why so many students fail to learn how to speak foreign languages is that they don't speak them enough. You cannot learn a language by looking at it.

The whole Japanese language is based on six key sounds which are the building blocks of two sets of syllables. These syllables never change, so once you learn how to pronounce them you can pronounce any word in the Japanese language. These six sounds and their pronunciations, as written in Roman letters, are *a* (ah), *i* (ee), *u* (uu), *e* (eh), *o* (oh), and *n,* pronounced as in the word "bond."

Note on Pronunciation

Here are all of the syllables making up the Japanese language, along with their English phonetic equivalents. Just pronounce the phonetics in standard English and the sounds will come out "in Japanese."

A	I	U	E	O
ah	ee	uu	eh	oh
KA	KI	KU	KE	KO
ka	kee	kuu	kay	koe
SA	SHI	SU	SE	SO
sa	she	sue	say	so
TA	CHI	TSU	TE	TO
tah	chee	t'sue	tay	toe
NA	NI	NU	NE	NO
nah	nee	nuu	nay	no
HA	HI	HU	HE	HO
hah	he	who	hay	hoe

MA	MI	MU	ME	MO
mah	me	moo	may	moe

YA	I	YU	E	YO
yah	ee	yuu	eh	yoe

RA	RI	RU	RE	RO
rah	ree	rue	ray	roe

(Roll the R's a bit)

*The "R" sound in Japanese is close to the "L" sound in English, which often requires a slight trilling sound to get it right.

GA	GI	GU	GE	GO
gah	ghee	goo	gay	go

ZA	ZI	ZU	ZE	ZO
zah	jee	zoo	zay	zoe

DA	JI	ZU	DE	DO
dah	jee	zoo	day	doe

BA	BI	BU	BE	BO
bah	bee	boo	bay	boe

PA	PI	PU	PE	PO
pah	pee	puu	pay	poe

*Note that the D and Z sounds are virtually the same in the case of ZI and JI.

The following syllables are combinations of some of those appearing above. The two primary syllables are

19

combined into one simply by merging the pronunciation.

RYA	RYU	RYO
re-yah	re-yuu	re-yoe
	(Roll the R's a bit)	
MYA	MYU	MYO
me-yah	me-yuu	me-yoe
NYA	NYU	NYO
ne-yah	ne-yuu	ne-yoe
HYA	HYU	HYO
he-yah	he-yuu	he-yoe
CHA	CHU	CHO
chah	chuu	choe
SHA	SHU	SHO
shah	shuu	show
KYA	KYU	KYO
q'yah	que	q'yoe
PYA	PYU	PYO
p'yah	p'yuu	p'yoe
BYA	BYU	BYO
b'yah	b'yuu	b'yoe
JA	JU	JO
jah	juu	joe
GYA	GYU	GYO
g'yah	g'yuu	g'yoe

When pronouncing the syllables in the second chart, keep in mind that they are to be pronounced as "one" syllable, not two. B'yuu, for example, should be run together; not pronounced as bee—you. In other words, as the "Beu" in "Beulah."

You should drill yourself on these pronunciation charts until you can enunciate each syllable easily and smoothly, without having to think about it. Before long you will be able to recognize individual syllables in the Japanese words you see and hear. The word *arigato* (thank you), for example, is made up of four syllables: *a-ri-ga-to* (ah-ree-gah-toe). Don't forget to trill the *ri* syllable a bit, as if it were Spanish. In fact, most of the single (uncombined) syllables in Japanese are pronounced almost exactly the same as Spanish. The A's are pronounced as ah's, the I's as ee's, and so on.

In Japanese the H and G letters are always pronounced hard, as in HO and GO. There are no true L or V sounds in Japanese, and they do not appear in the list of syllables. When the Japanese attempt to pronounce these letters in English words the L comes out as an R and V comes out as B.

Having been conditioned to pronounce words using only these syllables, the Japanese automatically render all English words into their own syllables—which is why "bread" becomes "bu-re-do" (buu-ray-doe) and "milk" becomes "mi-ru-ku" (me-rue-kuu). Of course, when the Japanese are speaking English, they try to pronounce English words in English and not in Japanese syllables.

More than 10,000 English words have been rendered into Japanese syllables, and are now a fundamental part of the language. Virtually every Japanese conversation is peppered with these adopted words, making the study and use of the language that much easier once you get used to the system. Of course, a Japanized English word may become meaningless to foreign ears if it is used out of context.

Again, the secret to using this book to communicate in Japanese is to pronounce the English phonetics for each word and sentence as standard English, practicing each sentence enough times that it comes out in a smooth flow. (Years ago it took me half an hour to get *Bakajanakaroka!* (Bah-kah-jah-nah-kah-roe-kah!) down pat. It means something like "Crazy S.O.B.!")

DEALING WITH GRAMMAR

The grammatical order of Japanese is subject, object, verb, instead of the subject, verb, object form of English. Having said that, I suggest that you ignore it for the time being (although this is probably the reason why the subject is often left out in Japanese conversation when the meaning is clear without it, and why the verb is often used by itself, playing the role of all the parts of speech). There is no definite or indefinite article (the, a) in Japanese, and there are very few plurals in the language. With few exceptions, the sense of plural is made evident by the context of the phrase or sentence. *Tokei* (toe-kay-e) means watch (time piece) or watches, depending on how it is used.

The "u" and the "i" are silent or are nearly so in the pronunciation of many words. For example, *desu,* which is the verb "to be," is pronounced as "dess." *Suki,* which means "like," is pronounced "ski." *Deshita,* which is the past tense of *desu* and means "was," is pronounced "desh-tah."

There are some words that have long vowels and some that have double consonants. The "o" sound in *koen,* meaning "park," is long, and is usually indicated in Romanized Japanese by a line above the letter. Some writers and publishers prefer to add a phonetic second letter after the long vowel as a pronunciation aid—"oo" or "oh," "aa," "ii." In ordinary conversation long vowels are often not really stressed that much but the meaning is clear from the context.

DOUBLE MEANINGS

Double consonants cannot be treated so lightly, however, as in many cases the meaning would be lost. Examples of words with double consonants are *Hokkaido,* pronounced "Hoke-kie-doe," and *kekko* (keck-

23

koe), meaning "wonderful" or "fine." The subordinate forms of many common verbs have double consonants, such as *atte* (aht-tay) from *au* meaning "meet," and *utte* (ute-tay) from *uru* meaning "sell." It is necessary to "hit" these clearly to be understood.

It is very easy to "make" the superlative in Japanese. All you do is put the word *ichiban* (ee-chee-bahn), meaning "first" or "number one" in front of the term you want to qualify. If big is *okii* (oh-kee), the biggest is *ichiban okii* (ee-chee-bahn oh-kee); the longest is *ichiban nagai* (ee-chee-bahn nah-guy); the smallest is *ichiban chiisai* (ee-chee-bahn chee-sie); the highest is *ichiban takai* (ee-chee-bahn tah-kie); the heaviest is *ichiban omoi* (ee-chee-bahn oh-moy); the best is *ichiban ii* (ee-chee-bahn ee), and so on.

In Japanese a question is indicated by the term *ka,* usually enunciated with the same "questioning" tone used in English, and in written Japanese this *ka* takes the place of the familiar question mark. I have chosen to write both the *ka* and the question mark to help make clear which sentences are questions.

HONORABLE "O's"

It is customary in Japanese to add an honorific "o" or "go" before many words that refer to other people, to things relating to others, and to certain special words, as a sign of respect or as a polite gesture.

In the sign-of-respect category are such words as *go-shujin* (go-shuu-jean), meaning "your honorable" husband; *o-taku* (oh-tah-kuu), meaning "your honorable" residence; *o-toshi* (oh-toe-she), "your honorable" age. The honorific "o" or "go" is also usually put before such words as temple (*o-tera* / oh-tay-rah), New Year's (*O-Shogatsu* / Oh-show-got-sue), accompany (*go-issho* / go-ees-show), guest (*o-kyaku* / oh-k'yah-kuu), and so on.

In the polite category are such words as weather (*o-tenki* / oh-ten-kee), saké or rice wine (*o-sake* / oh-sah-kay), wait (*o-machi* / oh-mah-chee), lunch box (*o-bento* / oh-ben-toe), and telephone (*o-denwa* / oh-den-wah).

In many cases, these "o" and "go" honorifics have more or less become a part of the words they precede and are generally included regardless of the circumstances.

The all important "I am; he/she is; we, you, they are" are all expressed in Japanese by *desu* (dess). The past tense of *desu,* expressing "I, he/she was; we, you, they were," is *deshita* (desh-tah).

There are three ways to express "there is" and "there are." When referring to human beings, use *orimasu* (oh-ree-mahss) for yourself or your family; (as it is a humble form); or *imasu* (ee-mahss), the neutral form, for anyone, you, your friends, etc. When referring to animals *imasu* (ee-mahss) is also used. When referring to inanimate objects, *arimasu* (ah-ree-mahss) is used. The past tense of these words are *orimashita* (oh-ree-mah-sshtah), *imashita* (ee-mah-sshtah) and *arimashita* (ah-ree-mah-sshtah).

PART ONE

1

Key Words

I   *Watakushi* (Wah-tock-she) — Slightly formal, used by both males and females
Watashi (Wah-tah-she) — Used more often by women than men
Boku (Boe-kuu) — Used by boys and men in informal situations
Ore (Oh-ray) — A "rough" term used by males in informal situations

ME   Any of the above terms used in the objective sense, in which case they are usually followed by a *ni* (nee), i.e.:
Watakushi ni (Wah-tock-she nee) — "To me," or "for me"
Boku ni (Boe-kuu nee)

MY   Any of the above "I" words followed by the indicator *no* (no), results in the possessive form. My book is *watakushi-no hon* (wah-tock-

	she-no hoan) or *boku-no hon* (boe-kuu no hoan)
WE	The "we" concept is formed by adding *tachi* (tah-chee) to any of the above forms of "I." *Watakushi-tachi* (Wah-tock-she-tah-chee); *boku-tachi* (boe-kuu-tah-chee)
YOU	*Anata* (Ah-nah-tah). The plural of you is formed by adding the suffix *gata* (gah-tah), which is polite, or *tachi* (tah-chee), which is standard: *Anata-gata* (Ah-nah-tah-gah-tah); *Anata-tachi* (Ah-nah-tah tah-chee). When used by women to address their husbands, *anata* is the equivalent of "dear."
YOUR	*Anata-no* (Ah-nah-tah-no). Your car *anata-no jidosha* (ah-nah-tah-no jee-doe-shah)
HE	*Anohito* (Ah-no-ssh-toe) or more polite, *anokata* (ah-no-kah-tah) Also the informal: *kare* (kah-ray)
HIS	*Anohito-no* (Ah-no-ssh-toe-no); *anokata-no* (ah-no-kah-tah-no); *kare-no* (kah-ray-no)
SHE	*Anokata* (Ah-no-kah-tah) or the informal *kano-jo* (kah-no-joe)
HERS	*Anokata-no* (Ah-no-kah-tah-no); *kano-jo-no* (kah-no-joe-no)

30

THEY   *Ano katagata* (ah-no kah-tah-gah-tah), or *ano hitotachi* (ah-no-ssh-toe-tah-chee)

THEIRS   *Anohito-tachi-no* (Ah-no-ssh-toe-tah-chee-no)

In informal conversation, he, she and they are frequently not used. The practice is to use the name of the individual concerned in order to be more specific and personal. It is also common practice to leave out "I" and "you" when the meaning is clear from the context, often subsuming the meaning in the verb form used. For example: Are you going? is often just expressed as: *Ikimasu ka?* (Ee-kee-mahss kah?) which technically means, "Going?" with the "you" understood. The usual answer would be *Ikimasu* (Ee-kee-mahss); or "Going," meaning, of couse, "I am going."

WHO   *Donata* (Doe-nah-tah); also the informal, *dare* (dah-ray)

WHOSE   *Donata-no* (Doe-nah-tah-no); *dare-no* (dah-ray-no)

WHAT   *Nani* (Nah-nee); shortened to *nan* (nahn) in sentences.

WHEN   *Itsu* (Eet-sue)

WHERE   *Doko* (Doe-koe)

WHY   *Naze* (Nah-zay); also: *doshite* (doe-ssh-tay)

HOW   *Doh* (Doh)

Yes *Hai* (Hie)

"Yes" is not used very often in Japanese to express affirmative agreement. The common practice is to repeat the positive form of whatever verb is used. For example if the question is: Do you understand? *Wakarimasu ka?* (Wah-kah-ree-mahss kah?) The most common answer is: *Wakarimasu* (wah-kah-ree-mahss) for "I understand" or *wakarimasen* (wah-kah-ree-mah-sen) for "I don't understand."

Hai is most often used to indicate "yes, I hear you," or "yes, I'm listening," particularly in telephone conversations.

No *Iie* (Ee-eh)

Iie is used more often to mean "no" than *hai* is to mean "yes," but the same practice generally applies. The negative of the verb or some other negative expression is more likely to be used in ordinary conversations. Japanese do not like to say "no" outright, and especially in business they usually couch the concept in more subtle forms.

The following words, presented here in their present, past, desiderative, negative, and present participle or subordinate forms, are commonly used with "to be"—*desu* (dess), with the subject (I, you, she, he and they) understood. To change them to the interrogative form (when you are referring to someone else) just add *ka* (kah) to the end.

Buy—*Kaimasu* (Kie-mahss) I buy. *Kaimashita* (Kie-mah-sshtah) I bought. *Kaitai* (Kie-tie) I want to buy. *Kaimasen* (Kie-mah-sen) I do not/will not buy. *Kaimasen deshita* (Kie-mah-sen desh-tah) I did not buy. *Kaitaku-nai* (Kie-tah-kuu-nie) I don't want to buy. *Katte kudasai* (Kot-tay kuu-dah-sie) Please buy. *Kaimasu ka?* (Kie-mahss kah?) Are you going to buy (it)?

Come—*Kimasu* (Kee-mahss) I come. *Kimashita* (Kee-mah-sshtah) I came. *Kitai* (Kee-tie) I want to come. *Kimasen* (Kee-mah-sen) I do not/will not come. *Kimasen deshita* (Kee-mah-sen desh-tah) I did not come. *Kitaku-nai* (Kee-tah-kuu-nie) I don't want to come. *Kite kudasai* (Kee-tay kuu-dah-sie) Please come. *Kimasu ka?* (Kee-mahss kah?) Are you coming?

Drink—*Nomimasu* (No-me-mahss) I drink. *Nomimashita* (No-me-mah-sshta) I drank. *Nomitai* (No-me-tie) I want to drink. *Nomimasen* (No-me-mah-sen) I do not/will not drink. *Nomimasen deshita* (No-me-mah-sen desh-tah) I did not drink. *Nomitaku-nai* (No-me-tah-kuu-nie) I don't want to drink. *Nonde kudasai* (Noan-day kuu-dah-sie) Please drink. *Nomimasu ka?* (No-me-mahss kah? Will you drink/Do you want to drink?)

Eat—*Tabemasu* (Tah-bay-mahss) I eat. *Tabemashita* (Tah-bay-mah-sshtah) I ate. *Tabetai* (Tah-bay-tie) I want to eat. *Tabemasen* (Tah-bay-mah-sen) I do not eat. *Tabemasen deshita* (Tah-bay-mah-sen desh-tah) I did not/will not eat. *Tabetaku-nae* (Tah-bay-tah-kuu-nie) I don't want to eat. *Tabete kudasai* (Tah-bay-tay kuu-dah-sie) Please eat. *Tabemasu ka?* (Tah-bay-mahss kah?) Will you eat/do you want to eat?

Forget—*Wasuremasu* (Wah-sue-ray-mahss) I forget. *Wasuremashita* (Wah-sue-ray-mah-sshtah) I forgot. *Wasuretai* (Wah-sue-ray-tie) I want to forget. *Wasuremasen* (Wah-sue-ray-mah-sen) I do not/will not forget. *Wasuremasen deshita* (Wah-sue-ray-mah-sen desh-tah) I did not forget. *Wasuretaku-nai* (Wah-sue-ray-tah-kuu-nie) I don't want to forget. *Wasurete kudasai* (Wah-sue-ray-tay kuu-dah-sie) Please forget.

Give—*Agemasu* (Ah-gay-mahss) I give. *Agemashita* (Ah-gay-mah-sshtah) I gave. *Agetai* (Ah-gay-tie) I want to give. *Agemasen* (Ah-gay-mah-sen) I do not/will not give. *Agemasen deshita* (Ah-gay-mah-sen desh-tah) I did not give. *Agetaku-nai* (Ah-gay-tah-kuu-nie) I do not want to give. *Agete kudasai* (Ah-gay-tay kuu-dah-sie) Please give (it to someone). *Agemasu ka?* (Ah-gay-mahss kah?) Will you give (it to someone)/shall I give (it to you)?

Go—*Ikimasu* (Ee-kee-mahss) I go. *Ikimashita* (Ee-kee-mah-sshtah) I went. *Ikitai* (Ee-kee-tie) I want to go. *Ikimasen* (Ee-kee-mah-sen) I am not going. *Ikimasen deshita* (Ee-kee-mah-sen desh-tah) I did not go. *Ikitaku-nai* (Ee-kee-tah-kuu-nie) I don't want to go. *Itte kudasai* (Eet-tay kuu-dah-sie) Please go. *Ikimasu ka?* (Ee-kee-mahss kah?) Are you/is she/he going?

Hear—*Kikimasu* (Kee-kee-mahss) I hear. *Kikimashita* (Kee-kee-mah-sshta) I heard. *Kikitai* (Kee-kee-tie) I want to hear. *Kikimasen* (Kee-kee-mah-sen) I do not/ did not hear. *Kikimasen deshita* (Kee-kee-mah-sen desh-tah) I did not hear. *Kikitaku-nai* (Kee-kee-tah-kuu-nie) I don't want to hear. *Kiite kudasai* (Keeee-tay kuu-dah-sie) Please listen. *Kikimasu ka?* (Kee-kee-mahss kah?) Do you hear/can you hear?

Have—*Motte imasu* (Moat-tay ee-mahss) I have. *Motte imashita* (Moat-tay ee-mah-sshtah) I had. *Motte imasen* (Moat-tay ee-mah-sen) I do not have. *Motte imasen deshita* (Moat-tay ee-mah-sen desh-tah) I did not have. *Motte imasu ka?* (Moat-tay ee-mahss kah?) Do you have (it)?

Know—*Shirimasu* (Ssh-ree-mahss) I know. *Shirimashita* (Ssh-ree-mah-sshtah) I knew. *Shiritai* (She-ree-tie) I want to know. *Shirimasen* (She-ree-mah-sen) I don't know. *Shiritaku-nai* (She-ree-tah-kuu-nie) I don't want to know. *Shitte imasu ka?* (Ssh-tay ee-mahss-kah?) Do you know?

Read—*Yomimasu* (Yoe-me-mahss) I read. *Yomimashita* (Yoe-me-mah-ssh-tah) I read. *Yomitai* (Yoe-me-tie) I want to read. *Yomimasen* (Yoe-me-mah-sen) I do not/will not read. *Yomimasen deshita* (Yoe-me-mah-sen desh-tah) I did not read. *Yomitaku-nai* (Yoe-me-tah-kuu-nie) I don't want to read. *Yonde kudasai* (Yoan-day kuu-dah-sie) Please read. *Yomimasu ka* (Yoe-me-mahss kah?) Will you read (it)?

Return—*Kaerimasu* (Kie-ree-mahss) I return. *Kaerima-shita* (Kie-ree-mahsshtah) I returned. *Kaeritai* (Kie-ree-tie) I want to return. *Kairimasen* (Kie-ree-mah-sen) I will not return. *Kaerimasen deshita* (Kie-ree-mah-sen desh-tah) I did not return. *Kaeritaku-nai* (Kie-ree-tah-kuu-nie) I do not want to return. *Kaette kudasai* (Kai-tay kuu-dah-sie) Please return. *Kaerimasu ka?* (Kie-ree-mahss kah?) Will you/he/she/they return?

Say—*Iimasu* (Eee-mahss) I say. *Iimashita* (Eee-mah-sshtah) I said. *Iitai* (Eee-tie) I want to say. *Iimasen* (Eee-mah-sen) I will not say. *Iimasen deshita* (Eee-mah-sen desh-tah) I did not say. *Iitaku-nai* (Eee-tah-kuu-nie) I don't want to say. *Itte kudasai* (Eet-tay kuu-dah-sie) Please say (it).

See—*Mimasu* (Me-mahss) I see. *Mimashita* (Me-mah-sshtah) I saw. *Mitai* (Me-tie) I want to see. *Mimasen* (Me-mah-sen) I do not/did not see. *Mimasen deshita* (Me-mah-sen desh-tah) I did not see. *Mitaku-nai* (Me-tah-ku-nie) I don't want to see. *Mite kudasai* (Me-tay kuu-dah-sie) Please look at it. *Mimasu ka?* (Me-mahss kah?) (Would you like to) see it?

Sleep—*Nemasu* (Nay-mahss) I sleep. *Nemashita* (Nay-mah-sshtah) I slept. *Netai* (Nay-tie) I want to sleep. *Nemasen* (Nay-mah-sen) I do not/will not sleep. *Nemasen deshita* (Nay-mah-sen desh-tah) I did not sleep. *Netaku-nai* (Nay-tah-kuu-nie) I don't want to sleep. *Nete kudasai* (Nay-tay kuu-dah-sie) Please sleep. *Nemasu ka?* (Nay-mahss kah?) Will you/do you want to sleep?

Speak—*Hanashimasu* (Hah-nah-she-mahss) I speak. *Hanashimashita* (Hah-nah-she-mah-sshtah) I spoke. *Hanashitai* (Hah-nah-she-tie) I want to speak. *Hanashimasen* (Hah-nah-she-mah-sen) I do not/will not speak. *Hanashimasen deshita* (Hah-nah-she-mah-sen desh-tah) I did not speak. *Hanashitaku-nai* (Hah-nah-she-tah-kuu-nie) I don't want to speak. *Hanashite kudasai* (Hah-nah-sshtay kuu-dah-sie) Please speak. *Hanashimasu ka* (Hah-nah-she-mahss kah?) Will you/he/she speak?

Understand—*Wakarimasu* (Wah-kah-ree-mahss) I understand. *Wakarimashita* (Wah-kah-ree-mah-sshtah) I understood. *Wakaritai* (Wah-kah-ree-tie) I want to understand. *Wakarimasen* (Wah-ak-ree-mah-sen) I don't understand. *Wakarimasen deshita* (Wah-kah-ree-mah-sen desh-tah) I did not understand. *Wakatte kudasai* (Wah-kot-tay kuu-dah-sie) Please understand. *Wakarimasu ka?* (Wah-kah-ree-mahss kah?) Do you understand?

Walk—*Arukimasu* (Ah-rue-kee-mahss) I walk. *Arukimashita* (Ah-rue-kee-mah-sshtah) I walked. *Arukitai* (Ah-rue-kee-tie) I want to walk. *Arukimasen* (Ah-rue-kee-mah-sen) I do not/will not walk. *Arukimasen deshita* (Ah-rue-kee-mah-sen desh-tah) I did not

walk. *Arukitaku-nai* (Ah-rue-kee-tah-kuu-nai) I don't
want to walk. *Aruite kudasai* (Ah-rue-ee-tay kuu-dah-
sie) Please walk. *Arukimasu ka?* (Ah-rue-kee-mahss
kah?) Will you/would you like to walk?

Wait—*Machimasu* (Mah-chee-mahss) I wait. *Machima-
shita* (Mah-chee-mah-sshtah) I waited. *Machitai* (Mah-
chee-tie) I want to wait. *Machimasen* (Mah-
chee-mah-sen) I do not/will not wait. *Machimasen
deshita* (Mah-chee-mah-sen desh-tah) I did not wait.
Machitaku-nai (Mah-chee-tah-kuu-nie) I don't want
to wait. *Matte kudasai* (Maht-tay kuu-dah-sie) Please
wait. *Machimasu ka?* (Mah-chee-mahss kah?) Will
you wait?

Write—*Kakimasu* (Kah-kee-mahss) I write. *Kakimashita*
(Kah-kee-mah-sshtah) I wrote. *Kakitai* (Kah-kee-tie)
I want to write. *Kakimasen* (Kah-kee-mah-sen) I do
not/will not write. *Kakimasen deshita* (Kah-kee-mah-
sen desh-tah) I did not write. *Kakitaku-nai* (Kah-kee-
tah-kuu-nie) I don't want to write. *Kaite kudasai*
(Kie-tay kuu-dah-sie) Please write. *Kakimasu ka?* (Kah-
kee-mahss-kah?) Will you write (it)/will you write
(to me)?

Common Phrases

Do you speak English?
Eigo wo hanashimasu ka?
(Aa-go oh hah-nah-she-mahss kah?)

I speak a little Japanese.
Nihon-go ga sukoshi hanasemasu
(Nee-hoan-go gah suu-koe-she hah-nah-say-mahss)

I don't understand.
Wakarimasen
(Wah-kah-ree-mah-sen)

Please say it again.
Mo ichido itte kudasai
(Moe ee-chee-doe eet-tay kuu-dah-sie)

Please speak more slowly.
Mo sukoshi yukkuri hanashite kudasai
(Moe suu-koe-shee yuke-kuu-ree hah-nah-sshtay
kuu-dah-sie)

I understood that.
Sore wa wakarimashita
(Soe-ray wah wah-kah-ree-mah-sshtah)

Did you understand?
Wakarimashita ka?
(Wah-kah-ree-mah-sshtah kah?)

I want to study Japanese.
Nihon-go wo benkyo shitai desu
(Nee-hoan-go oh ben-k'yoe she-tie dess)

39

Please speak in Japanese.
Nihon-go wo hanashite kudasai
(Nee-hoan-go oh hah-nah-ssh-tay kuu-dah-sie)

Is it all right?
Yoroshii desu ka?
(Yoe-roe-she dess kah?)

It's OK.
Daijobu desu
(Die-joe-buu dess)

Please.
Dozo; also, *onegaishimasu*
(Doe-zoe / oh-nay-guy-she-mahss)

It doesn't matter / I don't mind.
Kamaimasen
(Kah-my-mah-sen)

Is that so?
So desu ka?
(Soh dess kah?)

I don't want (need) it.
Irimasen
(Ee-ree-mah-sen)

I think so.
So omoimasu
(Soh oh-moy-ee-mahss)

I don't think so.
So omoimasen
(Soh oh-moy-mah-sen)

Not yet (used as a sentence).
Mada desu
(Mah-dah dess)

Just a moment.
Chotto matte
(Choat-toe mot-tay)

Chotto is also used by itself when you want to get someone's attention and/or call them to you—*Chotto!* (Choat-toe!). This is very familiar, however, and is primarily used among families and when addressing serving people in an informal setting, such as a restaurant.

When said in a reluctant, cautious tone of voice *chotto* means you don't want to respond to a question or comment, and are leaving it to the hearer to interpret your meaning. If someone says *chotto muzukashii* (choat-toe muu-zuu-kah-she), "it's a little difficult," they really mean it can't be done or they can't do it.

I've had enough / No more, thank you.
Mo kekko desu
(Moh keck-koe dess)

Well, I have to be going . . .
Sa! Soro-soro . . .
(Sah! So-roe-so-roe . . .)

Where did you study English?
Doko de Eigo wo benkyo shimashita ka?
(Doe-koe day Aa-go oh ben-k'yoe she-mah-sshta kah?)

Have you been to the United States?
Amerika e itta koto ga arimasu ka?
(Ah-may-ree-kah eh eet-tah koe-toe gah ah-ree-mahss kah?)

2

Greeting People

Good morning (said until about 10 a.m.).
Ohaiyo gozaimasu
(Oh-hie-yoe go-zie-mahss)

Good afternoon (said from around 10 a.m. until
about 5 p.m.).
Konnichi wa
(Kone-nee-chee wah)

Good evening (said from about 6 p.m. or around
dusk to midnight).
Komban wa
(Kome-bahn wah)

Goodnight.
Oyasumi nasai
(Oh-yah-sue-me nah-sie)

See you again tomorrow.
Mata ashita
(Mah-tah ah-ssh-tah)

How are you?
Ikaga desu ka?
(Ee-kah-gah dess kah?)

I'm fine.
Genki desu
(Gain-kee dess)

I'm fine, thanks to you (a set expression).

Okagesama de, genki desu
(Oh-kah-gay-sah-mah day, gain-kee dess)

It's been a long time, hasn't it!
O-hisashi buri desu, ne!
(Oh-he-sah-she-buu-ree dess, nay!)
or
Shibaraku deshita!
(Shee-bah-rah-kuu day day-ssh-tah!)

I've been out of touch for a long time!
Gobusata itashimashita!*
(Go-buu-sah-tah ee-tah-she-mah-ssh-tah!)

*This phrase is often used when meeting someone after having been out of touch for a long time and you feel a bit guilty.

Your wife	*Oku-san* (Oak-sahn)
My wife	*Kanai* (Kah-nie)
Your husband	*Go-shujin* (Go-shuu-jean)
My husband	*Shujin* (Shuu-jean)
Children	*Kodomo* (Koe-doe-moe)
Daughter	*Musume* (Muu-sue-may)
Son	*Musuko* (Muu-sue-koe)

How is your wife?
Oku-san wa ikaga desu ka?

44

(Oak-sahn wah ee-kah-gah dess kah?)

How is your husband?
Go-shujin wa ikaga desu ka?
(Go-shuu-jeen wah ee-kah-gah dess kah?)

She/he is well, thank you.
Arigato, genki desu
(Ah-ree-gah-toe, gain-kee dess)

How do you feel? (said to someone who has been ill
or down.)
Go-kigen wa ikaga desu ka?
(Go-kee-gen wa ee-kah-gah dess kah?)

I'm quite well, thank you.
Arigato, taihen genki desu
(Ah-ree-gah-toe, tie-hen gain-kee dess)

Welcome *Irasshaimase* (Ee-rah-shy-mah-say)*

*This is the polite, formal word commonly used in an
institutionalized way when welcoming people to your home,
etc. It is also the word that restaurant and bar staff
traditionally call out (loudly!) when new customers enter.
The more traditional the place of business, the louder and
more frequently the word is yelled out.

3

Introductions

Introduce	*Shokai suru* (Show-kie-sue-rue)
Letter of Introduction	*Shokaijo* (Show-kie-joe)
Name	*Namae* (Nah-my)—The similarity in spelling is coincidental
Name-card	*Meishi* (May-she)

May I introduce myself?
Jiko shokai shitemo ii desu ka?
(Jee-koe show-kie she-tay-moe ee dess kah?)

My name is De Mente.
Watakushi no namae wa De Mente desu
(Wah-tock-she no nah-my wah De Mente dess)

What is your name?
O-namae wa nan desu ka?
(Oh-nah-my wah nahn dess kah?)

Please introduce me to that man.

Ano otoko-no-hito ni shokai shite kudasai
(Ah-no oh-toe-koe-no-ssh-toe nee show-kie ssh-tay kuu-dah-sie)

I would like to introduce Mr. Tanaka.
Tanaka-san wo shokai shimasu
(Tah-nah-kah-sahn oh show-kie she-mahss)

I'm pleased to meet you.
Hajimemashite, dozo yoroshiku
(Hah-jee-may-mah-ssh-tay, doe-zoe yoe-roe-she-kuu)

This (person) is Mr. Adams.
Konokata wa Adams-san desu
(Koe-no-kah-tah wah Ah-dah-muu-sue-sahn dess)

Please accept my name-card.
Watakushi no meishi wo dozo
(Wah-tock-she no may-she oh doe-zoe)

May I have one of your name-cards?
Anata no meishi wo itadakimasen ka?
(Ah-nah-tah no may-she oh ee-tah-dah-kee-mah-sen kah?)

Please come in.
Dozo, o'hairi kudasai
(Doe-zoe, oh-hie-ree kuu-dah-sie)

Please sit down (especially Japanese-style on the floor).
Dozo, suwatte kudasai
(Doe-zoe, sue-wat-tay kuu-dah-sie)

Please sit down (on a chair).
Dozo, o-kake kudasai
(Doe-zoe, oh-kah-kay kuu-dah-sie)

Thank you very much. I'm really tired.
Domo arigato. Honto ni tsukaremashita
(Doe-moe ah-ree-gah-toe. Hoan-toe nee t'sue-kah-ray-mah-sshtah)

Don't mention it / You're welcome.
Do itashimashite
(Doe ee-tah-she-mah-sshtay)

4

In a Taxi

Left	*Hidari*	(He-dah-ree)
Right	*Migi*	(Me-ghee)
Straight	*Massugu*	(Mahss-sue-guu)
Intersection	*Kosaten*	(Koe-sah-ten)

Corner	*Kado* (Kah-doe)
Please turn	*Magatte kudasai* (Mah-got-tay kuu-dah-sie)
Please wait	*Matte kudasai* (Mot-tay kuu-dah-sie)
Address	*Jusho* (Juu-show)
In a hurry	*Isogimasu* (Ee-soe-ghee-mahss)

Please go to the Akasaka Prince Hotel.
Akasaka Purinsu Hoteru ni itte kudasai
(Ah-kah-sah-kah Puu-reen-sue Hoe-tay-rue nee eat-tay kuu-dah-sie)

Please go to Roppongi.
Roppongi ni itte kudasai
(Rope-pon-ghee nee eat-tay kuu-dah-sie)

also:

Roppongi made onegaishimasu
(Rope-pon-ghee mah-day oh-nay-guy-she-mahss)

Do you know the Nomura Securities Building?
Nomura Shoken Biru shitte imasu ka?
(No-muu-rah Show-ken Bee-rue ssh-tay ee-mahss kah?)

Please go to (place name).
(Place name) *ni itte kudasai*
([Place name] nee eet-tay kuu-dah-sie)

How many minutes is it to Shinjuku?
Shinjuku made nanpun gurai desu ka?
(Sheen-juu-kuu mah-day nahn poon guu-rye dess kah?)

Please stop at the next intersection.
Kono tsugi no kosaten de tomatte kudasai
(Koe-no t'sue-ghee no koh-sah-ten day toe-mot-tay kuu-dah-sie)

Turn left at the next corner.
Tsugi no kado de hidari e magatte kudasai
(T'sue-ghee no kah-doe day he-dah-ree eh mah-got-tay kuu-dah-sie)

Turn right here.
Koko de migi e magatte kudasai
(Koe-koe day me-ghee eh mah-got-tay kuu-dah-sie)

Please wait for me.
Matte kudasai
(Mot-tay kuu-dah-sie)

I'll be back in just two or three minutes.
Ni-san pun de kaerimasu
(Nee-sahn poon day kie-ree-mahss)

I want to go to this address.
Kono jusho ni ikitai desu
(Koe-no juu-show nee ee-kee-tie dess)

Please stop here.
Koko de tomete kudasai.
(Koe-koe day toe-may-teh kuu-dah-sie)

5

At a Hotel

Hotel	*Hoteru* (Hoe-tay-rue)
Front desk	*Furanto* (Fuu-rahn-toe)
Key	*Kagi* (Kah-ghee)
Reservations	*Yoyaku* (Yoe-yah-kuu)
Single	*Shinguru* (Sheen-guu-rue)
Double	*Daburu* (Dah-buu-rue)
Bed	*Betto* (Bet-toe)
Twin bed	*Tsuin betto* (T'sue-ween bet-toe)
Room rate	*Heya dai* (Hay-yah die)

Service charge	*Sabisu ryo* (Sah-bee-suu rio)
Air conditioning	*Reibo* (Ray-boe)
Room number	*Rumu namba* (Ruu-muu nahm-bah)
Checkout time	*Cheku-outo jikan* (Che-kuu-ow-toe jee-kahn)
Large	*Okii* (Oh-keee)
Small	*Chiisai* (Cheee-sie)
Coffee shop	*Kohi shoppu* (Koe-hee shope-puu)
Clean	*Kirei* (Kee-ray)
Blanket	*Mofu* (Moe-fuu)
Laundry	*Sentakumono* (Sen-tah-kuu-moe-no)
Emergency exit	*Hijo guchi* (He-joe guu-chee)
Chinese restaurant	*Chugoku ryori-ya* (Chuu-go-kuu rio-ree yah)
Drugstore	*Yakkyoku* (Yahk-k'yoe-kuu)
Beauty parlor	*Biyo in* (Bee yoeh een)
Business	*Shobai* (Show-by); also, *Bijinesu* (Bee-jee-nay-suu)
English newspaper	*Eibun no shimbun* (A-boon no sheem-boon)
Bell desk	*Beru desuku* (Bay-rue dess-kuu)
Cashier	*Kaikei* (Kie-kay)
Message	*Messeji* (Mays-say-jee); also, *kotozuke* (koe-toe-zuu-kay)

Shopping arcade   *Akeido* (Ah-kay-e-doe)

My name is Jones. I have a reservation.
Watakushi wa Jon-zuu desu. Yoyaku shite arimasu
(Wah-tock-she wah Joan-zuu dess. Yoe-yah-kuu ssh-
tay ah-ree-mahss)

What is my room number?
Watakushi no rumu namba wa nan ban desu ka?
(Wah-tock-she no ruu-muu nahm-bah wah nahn
bahn dess kah?)

Do you have a single?
Shinguru arimasu ka?
(Sheen-guu-ruu ah-ree-mahss kah?)

How about a double?
Daburu wa doh desu ka?
(Dah-buu-ruu wah doeh dess kah?)

How much is the room rate?
Heya dai wa ikura desu ka?
(Hay-yah die wah ee-kuu-rah dess kah?)

What time is checkout?
Cheku outo wa nan ji desu ka?
(Che-kuu ow-toe wah nahn jee dess kah?)

This room is too small.
Kono heya wa chiisai sugimasu
(Koe-no hay-yah wah cheee-sie suu-ghee-mahss)

Do you have a larger one?
Motto okii no arimasu ka?
(Moat-toe oh-keee no ah-ree-mahss kah?)

What time does the coffee shop open?
Kohi shoppu wa nanji ni akimasu ka?
(Koe-hee shope-puu wah nahn-jee nee ah-kay-mahss kah?)

Where is the coffee shop?
Kohi shoppu wa doko desu ka?
(Koe-hee shope-puu wah doe-koe dess kah?)

Please clean up my room.
Heya wo kirei ni shite kudasai
(Hay-yah oh kee-ray-e nee ssh-tay kuu-dah-sie)

I would like another blanket, please.
Mofu mo ichi-mae onegaishimasu
(Moe-fuu moe ee-chee-my oh-nay-guy-she-mahss)

Please wake me at 6 o'clock.
Roku ji ni okoshite kudasai

(Roe-kuu jee nee oh-koe-ssh-tay kuu-dah-sie)

Are there any messages for me?
Watakushi ni kotozuke ga arimasu ka?
(Wah-tock-she nee koe-toe-zuu-kay gah ah-ree-mahss kah?)

I have some laundry (for pick up).
Sentakumono ga arimasu
(Sen-tah-kuu-moe-no gah ah-ree-mahss)

When will it be ready?
Itsu dekimasu ka?
(Eet-sue day-kee-mahss kah?)

Can you extend my reservations?
Yoyaku wo nobasu koto ga dekimasu ka?
(Yoe-yah-kuu oh no-bah-suu koe-toe gah day-kee-mahss kah?)

I would like to stay for three more days.
Ato mikka tomaritai desu
(Ah-toe meek-kah toe-mah-ree-tie dess)

Please call me a taxi.
Takushi wo yonde kudasai
(Tock-she oh yoan-day kuu-dah-sie)

Can you recommend a Chinese restaurant?
Chugoku ryori-ya wo suisen (suru koto ga) dekimasu ka?
(Chuu-go-kuu rio-ree-yah oh sooey-sen (sue-rue koe-to gah) day-kee-mahss kah?)

How far is it from the hotel?
Hoteru kara dono kurai arimasu ka?
(Hoe-tay-rue kah-rah done-no kuu-rye ah-ree-mahss kah?)

Is there a pharmacy near the hotel?
Hoteru no chikaku ni yakkyoku ga arimasu ka?
(Hoe-tay-rue no chee-kah-kuu nee yack-k'yoe-kuu gah ah-ree-mahss kah?)

Can I walk there from the hotel?
Hoteru kara soko made arukemasu ka?
(Hoe-tay-rue kah-rah so-koe mah-day ah-ruu-kay-mahss kah?)

Where is your business service center?
Bijinesu sabisu senta wa doko desu ka?
(Bee-jee-nay-suu sah-bee-suu sen-tah wah doe-koe dess kah?)

Do you have secretarial service?
Hisho no sabisu ga arimasu ka?
(He-show no sah-bee-suu gah ah-ree-mahss kah?)

6

Asking Questions

American	*Amerika-jin* (Ah-may-ree-kah-jeen)
English person	*Eikoku-jin* (A-koe-kuu-jeen)
French person	*Furansu-jin* (Fuu-rahn-suu-jeen)
German person	*Doitsu-jin* (Doe-e-t'suu-jeen)
Chinese person	*Chugoku-jin* (Chuu-go-kuu-jeen)
Korean person	*Kankoku-jin* (Kahn-koe-kuu-jeen)
Canadian	*Kanada-jin* (Kah-nah-dah-jeen)
Japanese (person)	*Nihon-jin* (Nee-hoan-jeen)
Japanese language	*Nihon-go* (Nee-hoan-go)
Last name	*O-myoji* (Oh-me-oh-jee)
Leave	*Demasu* (Day-mahss)
Go out	*Dekakemasu* (Day-kah-kay-mahss)
Stop	*Tomarimasu* (Toe-mah-ree-mahss)
Meeting	*Kaigi* (Kie-ghee)
Japanese food	*Nihon ryori* (Nee-hoan rio-ree)

57

Western food   *Seiyo ryori* (Say-yoe rio-ree)
Chinese food   *Chugoku ryori* (Chuu-go-kuu
                                        rio-ree)

Who is it?
Donata desu ka?
(Doe-nah-tah dess kah?)

What is your last name?
O-myoji wa nan desu ka?
(Oh-me-oh-jee wah nahn dess kah?)

Are you Chinese?
Chugoku-jin desu ka?
(Chuu-go-kuu-jeen dess kah?)

No, I'm an American.
Iie, Amerika-jin desu
(Ee-eh, Ah-may-ree-kah-jeen dess)

What is your nationality?
Anato no kokuseki wa nan desu ka?
(Ah-nah-tah no koe-kuu-say-kee wah nahn dess
kah?)

What is that called in Japanese?
Sore wa Nihon-go de nan-to iimasu ka?

(Soe-ray wah Nee-hoan-go day nahn-toe ee-mahss kah?)

When are we/you/they leaving?
Itsu demasu ka? (note that the "we/you/they" is understood)
(Eet-sue day-mahss kah?)

Why have we stopped?
Naze tomarimashita ka?
(Nah-zay toe-mah-re-mah-sshtah kah?)

How shall we do it?
Do yu fu ni shimasho ka?
(Doh yuu fuu nee she-mah-show kah?)

Will he return soon?
Sugu kaerimasu ka?
(Sue-guu kie-ree-mahss kah?)

Is Mr. Tachibana coming to the meeting?
Tachibana-san wa kaigi ni kimasu ka?
(Tah-chee-bah-nah-sahn wah kie-ghee nee kee-mahss kah?)

Do you have to go now? / Do I/we have to go now?
Ima sugu ikanakereba narimasen ka?

(Ee-mah suu-guu ee-kah-nah-kay-ray-bah nah-ree-mah-sen ka?)

Will he come soon?
Sugu kimasu ka?
(Suu-guu kee-mahss kah?)

What is his rank/title?
Anohito no katagaki wa nan desu ka?
(Ah-no-ssh-toe no kah-tah-gah-kee wah nahn dess kah?)

What do you want to eat?
Nani wo tabetai desu ka?
(Nah-nee oh tah-bay-tie dess kah?)

Do you want to eat Japanese food?
Nihon no ryori wo tabetai desu ka?
(Nee-hoan no rio-ree oh tah-bay-tie dess kah?)

How about Western food?
Seiyo ryori wa doh desu ka?
(Say-yoe rio-ree wah doh dess kah?)

How about Chinese food?
Chugoku ryori wa ikaga desu ka?
(Chuu-goh-kuu rio-ree wah ee-kah-gah-dess kah?)

7

Going Somewhere

Cabaret	*Kyabare* (K'yah-bah-ray)
Bar	*Baa* (Bah)
Movie	*Eiga* (A-ee-gah)
Taxi	*Takushi* (Tock-she)
Subway	*Chikatetsu* (Chee-kah-tet-sue)
Sightseeing	*Kembutsu* (Kem-boot-sue)
Appointment	*Yakusoku* (Yahk-soe-kuu)
Far (distance)	*Toi* (Toy)
Close (nearby)	*Chikai* (Chee-kie)
Sushi restaurant	*Sushi ya* (Suu-shee yah)
Stroll, walk	*Sanpo* (Sahn-poe)

I want to go somewhere this evening.
Komban doko ka ni ikitai desu
(Kome-bahn doe-koe kah nee ee-kee-tie dess)

Wouldn't you like to go with me?
Issho ni ikimasen ka?
(Ees-show nee ee-kee-mah-sen kah?)

Let's go to a cabaret.
Kyabare ni ikimasho

(K'yah-bah-ray nee ee-kee-mah-show)

Where would you like to go?
Doko e ikitai no desu ka?
(Doe-koe eh ee-kee-tie no dess kah?)

I want to go to a sushi shop.
Sushi ya ni ikitai desu
(Sue-she yah nee ee-kee-tie dess)

I have to go to an appointment.
Yakusoku ni ikanakereba narimasen
(Yah-kuu-soe-kuu nee ee-kah-nah-kay-ray-bah nah-ree-mah-sen)

I'd like to do a little sightseeing.
Sukoshi kembutsu wo shitai no desu
(Sue-koe-she ken-boot-sue oh she-tie no dess)

Shall we go by subway?
Chikatetsu de ikimasu ka?
(Chee-kah-tet-sue day ee-kee-mahss kah?)

Let's go by taxi.
Takushi de ikimasho
(Tock-she day ee-kee-mah-show)

Is it far from here?

Koko kara toi desu ka?
(Koe-koe kah-rah toy dess kah?)

Is it near here?
Koko ni chikai desu ka?
(Koe-koe nee chee-kai dess kah?)

Is it near a subway station?
Chikatetsu no eki ni chikai desu ka?
(Chee-kah-tet-sue no a-kee nee chee-kie dess kah?)

Let's walk.
Arukimasho
(Ah-rue-kee-mah-show)

Let's take a walk.
Sanpo shimasho
(Sahn-poe she-mah-show)

8

The Cardinal Numbers

Numbers are vital to communication even on the most basic level. In Japanese there are two sets of cardinal numbers from 1 through

10, making it a bit more complicated than usual. One
set was borrowed from China and the other set is native
Japanese. From 11 on, the imported Chinese number-
ing system is used.

Japanese	Chinese
1 *hitotsu* (he-toe-t'sue)	1 *ichi* (ee-chee)
2 *futatu* (fuu-tah-t'sue)	2 *ni* (nee)
3 *mittsu* (meet-sue)	3 *san* (sahn)
4 *yottsu* (yoat-sue)	4 *shi* (she) or *yo* (yoe) or *yon* (yoan)
5 *itsutsu* (ee-t'sue-t'sue)	5 *go* (go)
6 *muttsu* (moot-sue)	6 *roku* (roe-kuu)
7 *nanatsu* (nah-naht-sue)	7 *shichi* (she-chee)
8 *yattsu* (yaht-sue)	8 *hachi* (hah-chee)
9 *kokonotsu* (koe-koe-no-t'sue)	9 *ku* (kuu) or *kyu* (que)
10 *to* (toe)	10 *ju* (juu)

Nanatsu is frequently abbreviated to *nana* (nah-nah).

The criterion for using these two sets of numbers is
fairly clear-cut. The Japanese set is generally used when
referring to units of 9 or under. For example, if you
want two orders of French fries you would not use *ni*
(2), but *futatsu*: *Furenchi furai wo futatsu kudasai* (Fuu-
rane-che fuu-rye oh fuu-tot-sue kuu-dah-sie). There are
occasions when numbers from 1–9 use the Chinese

numerals. These will be explained shortly in "Counting Things."

From 11 on all numbers are combinations of the Chinese set: 10 plus 1 = 11 and so on:

11	*ju-ichi*	(juu-ee-chee)
12	*ju-ni*	(juu-nee)
13	*ju-san*	(juu-sahn)
14	*ju-yon*	(juu-yoan)
15	*ju-go*	(juu-go)
16	*ju-roku*	(juu-roe-kuu)
17	*ju-shichi*	(juu-she-chee)
18	*ju-hachi*	(juu-hah-chee)
19	*ju-kyu*	(juu-que)
20	*ni-ju*	(nee-juu)
21	*ni-ju-ichi*	(nee-juu-ee-chee)
22	*ni-ju-ni*	(nee-juu-nee)
23	*ni-ju-san*	(nee-juu-sahn)
24	*ni-ju-shi*	(nee-juu-she)
25	*ni-ju-go*	(nee-juu-go)
30	*san-ju*	(sahn-juu)
31	*san-ju-ichi*	(sahn-juu-ee-chee)
40	*yon-ju*	(yoan-juu)
50	*go-juu*	(go-juu)
60	*roku-ju*	(roe-kuu-juu)
70	*nana-ju*	(nah-nah-juu)
80	*hachi-ju*	(hah-chee-juu)
90	*kyu-ju*	(que-juu)

100	*hyaku* (h'yah-kuu)
101	*hyaku-ichi* (h'yah-kuu-ee-chee)
102	*hyaku-ni* (h'yah-kuu-nee)
110	*hyaku-ju* (h'yah-kuu-juu)
111	*hyaku-ju-ichi* (h'yah-kuu-juu-ee-chee)
120	*hyaku-ni-ju* (h'yah-kuu-nee-juu)
130	*hyaku-san-ju* (h'yah-kuu-sahn-juu)
150	*hyaku-go-ju* (h'yah-kuu-go-juu)
200	*ni-hyaku* (nee-h'yah-kuu)
300	*sam-byaku* (sahm-b'yah-ku)
400	*yon-hyaku* (yoan-h'yah-kuu)
500	*go-hyaku* (go-h'yah-kuu)
600	*rop-pyaku* (rope-p'yah-kuu)
700	*nana-hyaku* (nah-nah-h'yah-kuu)
800	*hap-pyaku* (hop-p'yah-kuu)
900	*kyu-hyaku* (que-h'yah-kuu)
1,000	*sen* or *issen* (sen) or (ees-sen)
1,500	*sen-go-hyaku* (sen-go-h'yah-kuu)
2,000	*ni-sen* (nee-sen)
2,700	*ni-sen-nana-hyaku* (nee-sen-nah-nah-h'yah-kuu)
2,900	*ni-sen-kyu-hyaku* (nee-sen-que-h'yah-kuu)
3,000	*san-zen* (sahn zen)- note occasional euphonic changes to make pronunciation easier
4,000	*yon-sen* (yoan-sen)
5,000	*go-sen* (go-sen)
9,000	*kyu-sen* (que-sen)

10,000	*ichi-man* (ee-chee-mahn)
11,000	*ichi-man-issen* (ee-chee-mahn-ees-sen)
12,000	*ichi-man-ni-sen* (ee-chee-mahn-nee-sen)
15,000	*ichi-man-go-sen* (ee-chee-mahn-go-sen)
20,000	*ni-man* (nee-mahn)
25,000	*ni-man-go-sen* (nee-mahn-go-sen)
30,000	*san-man* (sahn-mahn)
40,000	*yon-man* (yoan-mahn)
50,000	*go-man* (go-mahn)
80,000	*hachi-man* (hah-chee-mahn)
100,000	*ju-man* (juu-mahn)
150,000	*ju-go-man* (juu-go-mahn)
175,500	*ju-nana-man-go-sen-go-hyaku* (juu-nah-nah-mahn-go-sen-go-h'yah-kuu)
200,000	*ni-ju-man* (nee-juu-mahn)
300,000	*san-ju-man* (sahn-juu-mahn)
500,000	*go-ju-man* (go-juu-mahn)
1,000,000	*hyaku man* (h'yah-kuu-mahn)
1,500,500	*hyaku-go-ju-man-go-hyaku* (h'yah-kuu-go-juu-mahn-go-h'yah-kuu)
2,000,000	*ni-hyaku man* (nee-h'yah-kuu-mahn)
3,000,000	*san-byaku man* (sahn-b'yah-kuu-mahn)
4,000,000	*yon-hyaku man* (yoan-h'ya-kuu-mahn)
5,000,000	*go-hyaku man* (go-h'ya-kuu–mahn)
6,000,000	*rop-pyaku man* (rope-p'ya-kuu–mahn)
10,000,000	*issen man* (ees-sen-mahn)
15,000,000	*issen go-hyaku man* (ees-sen go-h'ya-kuu-mahn)

9

The Ordinal Numbers

Converting cardinal numbers to ordinal numbers is simple. All you do is add *bamme* to the cardinal numbers. In usage, *bamme* is often shortened to *ban*. For example: What number are you? *Anata wa nan ban desu ka?* (Ah-nah-tah wah nahn bahn dess kah?) I'm number five. *Go-ban desu* (Go-bahn dess).

1st	*ichi-bamme*	(ee-chee-bahm-may)
2nd	*ni-bamme*	(nee-bahm-may)
3rd	*san-bamme*	(sahn-bahm-may)
4th	*yon-bamme*	(yoan-bahm-may)
5th	*go-bamme*	(go-bahm-may)
10th	*ju-bamme*	(juu-bahm-may)
20th	*ni-ju-bamme*	(nee-juu-bahm-may)
50th	*go-ju-bamme*	(go-juu-bahm-may)

The prefix *dai* (die) may be put in front of ordinal numbers to emphasize the order of things. For example: "the first one" could be *ichi-bamme* (ee-chee-bahm-may) or *dai-ichi-bamme* (die-ee-chee-bahm-may). When the ordinal number qualifies a noun, the particle *no* is used to connect them. "The second person" is *ni-bamme no hito* (nee-bahm-may no ssh-toe).

10

Counting Things

A special set of numeratives is used when counting things and people in Japanese. Altogether there are over 25 such numeratives. The most commonly used ones for things are *hiki* (hee-kee) used when counting animals, fish and insects; *wa* (wah) used when counting birds; *satsu* (sot-sue) used when counting books; *hon* (hoan) used when counting round, long objects such as pencils, fingers, trees, chopsticks, poles, legs, and so on; *mai* (my) used when counting flat things such as paper, sheets, dishes, boards, trays, and the like; and *hai* (hie), used to designate cups or glassfuls of water or other liquids.

Two dogs — *Ni-hiki no inu* (Nee-hee-kee no ee-nuu)
Three birds — *San-wa no tori* (Sahn-wah no toe-ree)
Two pencils — *Ni-hon no empitsu* (Nee-hoan no emm-peet-sue)
Five sheets of paper — *Go-mai no kami* (Go-my no kah-me)
Three books — *San-satsu no hon* (Sahn-sot-sue no hoan)
Two glasses of water — *Ni-hai no mizu* (Nee-hie no me-zuu)

Please bring me two sheets of paper.
Kami wo ni-mai motte kite kudasai
(Kah-me oh nee-my moat-tay kee-tay kuu-dah-sie)

I have lost two books.
Ni-satsu no hon wo nakushimashita
(Nee-sot-sue no hoan oh nah-kuu-she-mah-ssh-tah)

I want to buy only one book.
Hon wo i-satsu dake kaitai desu
(Hoan oh ee-sot-sue dah-kay kie-tie dess)

Two glasses of water, please.
Mizu wo ni-hai kudasai
(Me-zuu oh nee-hie kuu-dah-sie)

Again, when counting or ordering something like hamburgers, which have a more or less indefinite shape, it is common to use the Japanese set of numerals—*hitotsu, futatsu, mittsu*. For example:

Two hamburgers, please.
Hambaga wo futatsu kudasai
(Hahm-bah-gah oh fuu-tot-sue kuu-dah-sie)

If you don't know the correct numerative for whatever is concerned, just use numbers from either of the two sets (Japanese or Chinese). It will sound odd but you will be understood.

11

Counting People

There are two numeratives—*nin* (neen) and *mei* (may) for counting people and a special form of *hitotsu* (1) and *futatsu* (2) for counting one person and two people. Taking these two special forms first, they are *hitori* (he-toe-ree) meaning one person and *futari* (fuu-tah-ree), meaning two people. These special words are generally used instead of either of the two numeratives when referring to one person or two people.

The *mei* numerative seems to be mostly used when counting the number of people in dining groups arriving at restaurants. The host or waiter will commonly ask, *Nan-mei sama desu ka?* (Nahn-may sah-mah dess ka?) or "How many people?" of each new party or group that appears.

In responding to this question it is common to use *hitori* or *futari* if there is one or two, and the numerative *nin* if there is more—i.e. *San-nin desu* (Sahn-neen dess) or "Three people"; *Roku-nin desu* (Roe-kuu-neen dess) or "Six people."

In all general references to three or more people the *nin* (neen) numerative is used. Five people is *go-nin*. Ten people is *ju-nin*. Fifteen people is *ju-go-nin*.

I/we have reservations for five people.
Go-nin no yoyaku wo shite arimasu
(Go-neen no yoe-yah-kuu oh ssh-tay ah-ree-mahss)

12

Time Frames

Today	*Kyo* (K'yoe)
This afternoon	*Kyo gogo* (K'yoe go-go)
This evening	*Kyo no yoru* (K'yoe no yoe-rue)
Tonight	*Komban* (Kome-bahn)
Tomorrow	*Ashita* (Ah-ssh-tah)
Tomorrow morning	*Ashita no asa* (Ah-ssh-tah no ah-sah)
Tomorrow afternoon	*Ashita no gogo* (Ah-ssh-tah no go-go)
Day after tomorrow	*Asatte* (Ah-sot-tay)

Yesterday	*Kino* (Kee-no)
Day before yesterday	*Ototoi* (Oh-toe-toy)
Day (generic)	*Nichi* (Nee-chee)
Last night	*Yube* (You-bay)
Every day	*Mai nichi* (My nee-chee)
Every night	*Mai ban* (My bahn)
Every other day	*Mai nichi oki* (My nee-chee oh-kee)
From today	*Kyo kara* (K'yoe kah-rah)
From tomorrow	*Ashita kara* (Ah-ssh-tah kah-rah)
In the morning/a.m.	*Gozen* (Go-zen)
In the afternoon/p.m.	*Gogo* (Go-go)

What day is today?
Kyo wa nan nichi desu ka?
(K'yoe wah nahn nee-chee dess kah?)

I will be in Tokyo only three days.
Mikka dake Tokyo ni orimasu
(Meek-kah dah-kay Tokyo nee oh-ree-mahss)

Tomorrow I want to meet Mr. Suzuki.
Ashita Suzuki-san ni aitai desu
(Ah-ssh-tah Suu-zuu-kee-sahn nee aye-tie dess)

Please meet me today.
Kyo atte kudasai

(K'yoe aht-tay kuu-dah-sie)

Yesterday I ate sushi.
Kino sushi wo tabemashita
(Kee-no suu-she oh tah-bay-mah-sshtah)

Last night I went to a karaoke bar.
Yube karaoke baa ni ikimashita
(You-bay kah-rah-oh-kay bah nee ee-kee-mah-sshtah)

I really enjoyed yesterday.
Kino wa honto ni tanoshikatta
(Kee-no wah hoan-toe nee tah-no-she-kah-tah)

Where are we/you going day after tomorrow?
Asatte wa doko e ikimasu ka?
(Ah-sot-tay wah doe-koe eh ee-kee-mahss kah?)

13

The Days

The days of the week follow the same pattern as in English, with the last syllable in each word, *bi* (bee), meaning "day." *Bi* is also pronounced *hi* (he) and *nichi* (nee-chee), depending on the use.

Monday	*Getsuyobi* (Get-sue-yoe-bee)
Tuesday	*Kayobi* (Kah-yoe-bee)
Wednesday	*Suiyobi* (Sooey-yoe-bee)
Thursday	*Mokuyobi* (Moe-kuu-yoe-bee)
Friday	*Kin-yobi* (Keen-yoe-bee)
Saturday	*Doyobi* (Doe-yoe-bee)
Sunday	*Nichiyobi* (Nee-chee-yoe-bee)

Today is Monday.
Kyo wa Getsuyobi desu
(K'yoe wah Get-sue-yoe-bee dess)

Tomorrow will be Tuesday.
Ashita wa Kayobi desu
(Ah-ssh-tah wah Kah-yoe-bee dess)

The day after tomorrow will be Wednesday.
Asatte wa Suiyobi desu
(Ah-sot-tay wah Sooey-yoe-bee dess)

I am going to Kyoto on Thursday.
Mokuyobi ni Kyoto e ikimasu
(Moe-kuu-yoe-bee nee K'yoe-toe eh ee-kee-mahss)

I will return to Tokyo on Friday.
Kin-yobi ni Tokyo e kaerimasu
(Keen-yoe-bee nee Tokyo eh kie-ree-mahss)

On Saturday I'm going to meet a friend.
Doyobi ni tomodachi ni aimasu
(Doe-yoe-bee nee toe-moe-dah-chee nee aye-mahss)

On Sunday I'm going to see a movie.
Nichiyobi ni eiga wo mi ni ikimasu
(Nee-chee-yoe-bee nee aa-ee-gah oh me nee ee-kee-mahss)

What day is today?
Kyo wa nan yobi desu ka?
(K'yoe wah nahn yoe-bee dess kah?)

14

Counting Days

When referring to one or more days, just add *nichi* (nee-chee) to the appropriate number. *Nichi* by itself means "day."

one day   *ichi nichi* (ee-chee nee-chee)

two days	*ni nichi* (nee nee-chee)
	futsuka (fuu-tsue-kah)
three days	*san nichi* (sahn nee-chee)
	mikka (meek-kah)
eight days	*hachi nichi* (hah-chee nee-chee)
ten days	*ju nichi* (juu nee-chee)
	toka (toe-kah)
twenty-five days	*ni-ju-go nichi* (nee-juu-go nee-chee)
twenty-eight days	*ni-ju-hachi nichi* (nee-juu-hah-chee nee-chee)

How many days are you going to be here?
Nan nichi gurai koko ni imasu ka?
(Nahn nee-chee guu-rye koe-koe nee ee-mahss kah?)

I/we will be in Tokyo for six days
Roku nichi ni Tokyo ni imasu
(Roe-kuu nee-chee nee Tokyo nee ee-mahss)

How many days will it take?
Nan nichi gurai kakarimasu ka?
(Nahn nee-chee guu-rye kah-kah-ree-mahss kah?)

It will take three days.
San nichi kakarimasu
(Sahn nee-chee kah-kah-ree-mahss)

15

The Weeks

Japanese for week is *shu* (shuu or shoe). To express the concept of one week's time, the suffix *kan* (kahn) is added to *shu*—i.e. *shu-kan* means week, weeks, or weekly. Add a "one" as a prefix—*i-shu-kan* (ee-shuu-kahn) and you have "one week." Two weeks is, of course, *ni-shu-kan* (nee-shuu-kahn) and three weeks is *san-shu-kan* (sahn-shuu-kahn).

This week	*Kon shu* (Kone shuu)
Next week	*Rai shu* (Rye shuu)
Last week	*Sen shu* (Sen shuu)
Week after next	*Sa rai shu* (Sah rye shuu)
Week before last	*Sen sen shu* (Sen sen shuu)
Weekday	*Hei-nichi* (Hay-ee nee-chee); *hei-jitsu* (hay-jee-t'sue)
Weekend	*Shu-matsu* (Shuu-mot-sue)

Will this be ready by next week?
Kore wa rai shu made dekimasu ka?
(Koe-ray wah rye shuu mah-day day-kee-mahss kah?)

Please wait until the week after next.

Sa rai shu made matte kudasai
(Sah rye shuu mah-day mot-tay kuu-dah-sie)

I will be in Tokyo until next week.
Rai shu made Tokyo ni orimasu
(Rye shuu mah-day Tokyo nee oh-ree-mahss)

Altogether, I will be here for three weeks.
Zembu de san shu-kan koko ni orimasu
(Zem-buu day sahn shuu-kahn koe-koe nee oh-ree-mahss)

How many weeks have you been in the U.S.?
Nan shu-kan Amerika ni imashita ka?
(Nahn shuu-kahn Ah-may-ree-kah nee ee-mah-sshtah kah?)

16

Counting Weeks

As mentioned earlier, weeks are counted by adding a numeral prefix to *shukan* (with some euphonic changes to make pronunciation easier):

one week	*i-sshukan* (ee-shuu-kahn)
two weeks	*ni-shukan* (nee-shuu-kahn)
three weeks	*san-shukan* (sahn-shuu-kahn)
four weeks	*yon-shukan* (yoan-shuu-kahn)
five weeks	*go-shukan* (go-shuu-kahn)
six weeks	*roku-shukan* (roak-shuu-kahn)
seven weeks	*nana-shukan* (nah-nah-shuu-kahn)
eight weeks	*ha-sshukan* (hah-shuu-kahn)
nine weeks	*kyu-shukan* (que-shuu-kahn)
ten weeks	*jisshukan* (jee-shuu-kahn)
eleven weeks	*ju-isshukan* (juu-ee-shuu-kahn)

Two weeks ago.
Ni-shukan mae ni
(Nee-shuu-kahn my nee)

Four weeks ago.
Yon-shukan mae
(Yoan-shuu-kahn my)

Two more weeks.
Ato ni-shukan
(Ah-toe nee-shuu-kahn)

Will the rain continue for three more weeks?
Ame wa ato san-shukan tsuzukimasu ka?
(Ah-may wah ah-toe sahn-shuu-kahn t'sue-zuu-kee-mahss kah?)

17

The Months

Japanese for month is *gatsu* (got-sue) when used in a general sense, and *getsu* (get-sue) when expressing month-long periods of time. To name the months of the year just add the numbers one through twelve:

January	*Ichigatsu* (Ee-chee-got-sue)
February	*Nigatsu* (Nee-got-sue)
March	*Sangatsu* (Sahn-got-sue)
April	*Shigatsu* (She-got-sue)
May	*Gogatsu* (Go-got-sue)
June	*Rokugatsu* (Roe-kuu-got-sue)
July	*Shichigatsu* (She-chee-got-sue)
August	*Hachigatsu* (Hah-chee-got-sue)
September	*Kugatsu* (Kuu-got-sue)
October	*Jugatsu* (Juu-got-sue)
November	*Juichigatsu* (Juu-ee-chee-got-sue)
December	*Junigatsu* (Juu-nee-got-sue)
This month	*Kon getsu* (Kone get-sue)
Next month	*Rai getsu* (Rye get-sue)
Last month	*Sen getsu* (Sen get-sue)
Month after next	*Sa rai getsu* (Sah rye get-sue)

| Month before last | *Sen sen getsu* (Sen sen get-sue) |
| Monthly | *Gekkan* (Gek-kahn)—note spelling change for pronunciation |

Will the weather get better next month?
Rai getsu ni wa o-tenki ga yoku narimasu ka?
(Rye get-sue nee wah oh-ten-kee gah yoe-kuu nah-ree-mahss kah?)

My birthday was last month.
Watakushi no tanjobi wa sen getsu deshita
(Wah-tock-she no tahn-joe-bee wah sen get-sue desh-tah)

Is this magazine monthly?
Kono zasshi wa gekkan desu ka?
(Koe-no zah-she wah gek-kahn dess kah?)

18

Counting Months

Months are counted by combining the numeral, "ka" and "month."

one month   *ik-ka-getsu* (eek-kah-get-sue)

two months	*ni-ka-getsu* (nee-kah-get-sue)
three months	*san-ka-getsu* (sahn-kah-get-sue)
four months	*yon-ka-getsu* (yoan-kah-get-sue)
five months	*go-ka-getsu* (go-kah-get-sue)
six months	*rok-ka-getsu* (roak-kah-get-sue)
seven months	*nana-ka-getsu* (nah-nah-kah-get-sue)
eight months	*hachi-ka-getsu* (hah-chee-kah-get-sue)
nine months	*kyu-ka-getsu* (que-kah-get-sue)
ten months	*juk-ka-getsu* (juu-kah-get-sue)
eleven months	*ju-ichi-ka-getsu* (juu-ee-chee-kah-get-sue)
twelve months	*ju-ni-ka-getsu* (juu-nee-kah-get-sue)

How many months have you been here?
Nan ka-getsu gurai koko ni imashita ka?
(Nahn kah-get-sue guu-rye koe-koe nee ee-mah-sshtah kah?)

I/we've been in Japan for five months.
Go-ka-getsu Nihon ni imashita
(Go-kah-get-sue Nee-hoan nee ee-mahssh-tah)

This project will take two months.
Kono kigyo wa ni-ka-getsu kakarimasu
(Koe-no kee-g'yoe wah nee kah get-sue kah-kah-ree-mahss)

83

19

Giving Dates

A special word, *tsuitachi* (t'sue-ee-tah-chee), is used for the 1st or "first" day of the month. For example, April 1st is *Shigatsu no tsuitachi* (She-got-sue no t'sue-ee-tah-chee). From the 2nd through the 10th the native Japanese pronunciation of the numbers is used with yet another way of reading *nichi* or "day," in this case *ka*.

1st (of the month)	*tsuitachi*	(t'sue-ee-tah-chee)
2nd "	*futsu-ka*	(fuu-t'sue-kah)
3rd "	*mik-ka*	(meek-kah)
4th "	*yok-ka*	(yoke-kah)
5th "	*itsu-ka*	(ee-t'sue-kah)
6th "	*mui-ka*	(muu-ee-kah)
7th "	*nano-ka*	(nah-no-kah)
8th "	*yo-ka*	(yoh-kah)
9th "	*kokono-ka*	(koe-koe-no-kah)
10th "	*to-ka*	(toh-kah)

In addition, the 14th and 24th follow the same rule (juu-yoke-ka; nee-juu-yoke-ka), and the 20th has a special reading, *hatsu-ka* (hah-t'sue-kah). Otherwise, the rest of the days use the Chinese pronunciation of the numbers along with nichi for "day." If you forget, don't worry. The Chinese pronunciation for any of these days is perfectly understandable. So, for example, if you call the 20th *ni-ju-nichi* (nee-juu-nee-chee), you will still be understood.

11th	"	*ju-ichi-nichi*	(juu-ee-chee-nee-chee)
12th	"	*ju-ni-nichi*	(juu-nee-nee-chee)
13th	"	*ju-san-nichi*	(juu-sahn-nee-chee)
14th	"	*ju-yokka*	(juu-yoke-kah)
15th	"	*ju-go-nichi*	(juu-go-nee-chee)
18th	"	*ju-hachi-nichi*	(juu-hah-chee nee-chee)
20th	"	*hatsu-ka*	(hah-t'sue-kah)
21st	"	*ni-ju-ichi-nichi*	(nee-juu-ee-chee-nee-chee)
26th	"	*ni-ju-roku-nichi*	(nee-juu-roe-kuu-nee-chee)
30th	"	*san-ju-nichi*	(sahn-juu-nee-chee)

We are going to Osaka on the 21st.
Ni-ju-ichi-nichi ni Osaka e ikimasu
(Nee-juu-ee-chee-nee-chee nee Oh-sah-kah eh ee-kee-mahss)

Tomorrow will be the 6th.

Ashita wa muika desu
(Ah-ssh-tah wah muu-ee-kah dess)

We leave on the 18th.
Ju-hachi-nichi ni kaerimasu
(Juu-hah-chee nee-chee nee kie-ree-mahss)

Will it get hot in August?
Hachigatsu ni atsuku narimasu ka?
(Hah-chee-got-sue nee aht-sue-kuu nah-ree-mahss kah?)

I am going to Japan in April.
Shigatsu ni Nihon e ikimasu
(She-got-sue nee Nee-hone eh ee-kee-mahss)

Please respond/reply by July 15th.
Shichigatsu no ju-go-nichi made ni henji wo shite kudasai
(She-chee-got-sue no juu-go-nee-chee mah-day nee hen-jee oh ssh-tay kuu-dah-sie)

Today is the 28th of November.
Kyo wa juichigatsu no ni-ju-hachi-nichi desu
(K'yoe wah juu-ee-chee-got-sue no nee-juu-hah-chee-nee-chee dess)

I will return next month.
Rai getsu modorimasu

(Rye get-sue moe-doe-ree-mahss)

A few months
Su-ka-getsu
(Sue-kah-get-sue)

Every month
Mai tsuki
(My t'sue-kee)

20

The Years

Year	*Toshi* (Toe-she); also, *nen* (nen)
This year	*Ko toshi* (Koe toe-she)
Last year	*Kyo nen* (K'yoe nen)
Next year	*Rai nen* (Rye nen)
Every year	*Mai toshi* (My toe-she)
Year round	*Ichi nen ju* (Ee-chee nen juu)
Yearly income	*Nen shu* (Nen shuu)
New Year's Eve	*O-Mi soka* (Oh-Me Soh-kah)
New Year's	*O-Shogatsu* (Oh-Show-got-sue)

New Year's Day	*Gan Jitsu* (Ghan Jeet-sue)
Happy New Year	*Shin Nen O-medeto Gozaimasu* (Sheen Nen Oh-May-day-toe Go-zie-mahss
For one year	*Ichi nen kan* (Eee-chee nen kahn)
For two years	*Ni nen kan* (Nee nen kahn)
For three years	*San nen kan* (Sahn nen kahn)
For five and a half years	*Go nen kan han* (Go nen kahn hahn)

I have studied Japanese for one year.
Ichi nen kan Nihon-go wo benkyo shimashita
(Ee-chee nen kahn Nee-hoan-go oh ben-k'yoe she-mah-sshtah)

Japan now uses two systems for counting years, the Western system and their own traditional system of figuring years on the basis of the reign of the current emperor. The reign of each emperor is given a name, such as Meiji and Showa, and thereafter years are counted as the 30th year of Showa, the 3rd year of *Heisei* (Hay-say), and so on—*Showa san-ju-nen* (Show-wah sahn-juu-nen), *Heisei san-nen* (Hay-say sahn-nen). Younger people seem to be more familiar with the Western system.

1990 *Sen kyu-hyaku kyu-ju nen* (Sen que-h'yah-kuu que-juu nen)

1991 *Sen kyu-hyaku kyu-ju-ichi nen* (Sen que-h'yah-kuu que-juu-ee-chee nen)

1995 *Sen kyu-hyaku kyu-ju-go nen* (Sen que-h'yah-kuu que-juu-go nen)

2000 *Ni-sen nen* (Nee-sen nen)

2005 *Ni-sen go nen* (Nee-sen go nen)

2010 *Ni-sen ju nen* (Nee-sen juu nen)

He was born in 1970.

Anohito wa sen kyu hyaku nana ju nen ni umaremashita (Ah-no-ssh-toe wah sen que h'yah-kuu nah-nah juu nen nee uu-mah-ray-mah-sshtah)

21

The Seasons

Spring	*Haru* (Hah-rue)
Summer	*Natsu* (Not-sue)
Fall	*Aki* (Ah-kee)

Winter	*Fuyu* (Fuu-yuu)
Season	*Kisetsu* (Kee-set-sue)

When does spring start?
Haru wa itsu kara desu ka?
(Hah-rue wah eet-sue kah-rah dess kah?)

The weather is fine in the fall.
Aki wa tenki ga ii desu
(Ah-kee wah ten-kee gah ee dess)

22

The Time

In Japanese "minute" is *fun* (foon) or *pun* (poon), time in a generic sense (o'clock) is *ji* (jee), and a duration of time (or "hour") is *ji* plus *kan* or *jikan* (jee-kahn). These combined with numbers give us the time. There are slight euphonic changes in the spellings to accommodate pronunciation.

One minute	*Ip pun* (Eep-poon)
Two minutes	*Ni fun* (Nee Foon)
Three minutes	*San pun* (Sahn poon)
Four minutes	*Yon pun* (Yone poon)

Five minutes	*Go fun* (Go foon)
Six minutes	*Rop pun* (Rope poon)
Seven minutes	*Nana fun* (Hah-nah foon)
Eight minutes	*Hachi fun* (Hah-chee foon)
Nine minutes	*Kyu fun* (Que foon)
Ten minutes	*Jip pun* (Jeep-poon)
Eleven minutes	*Ju-ip pun* (Juu-eep poon)
Twelve minutes	*Ju-ni fun* (Juu-nee foon)
Fifteen minutes	*Ju-go fun* (Juu-go foon)
Twenty minutes	*Ni-jip pun* (Nee-jeep poon)
Thirty minutes	*San-jip pun* (Sahn-jeep poon)
Forty minutes	*Yon-jip pun* (Yone-jeep poon)
Fifty minutes	*Go-jip pun* (Go-jeep poon)
One hour	*Ichi jikan* (Ee-chee jee-kahn)
Two hours	*Ni jikan* (Nee jee-kahn)
Three hours	*San jikan* (Sahn jee-kahn)
Four hours	*Yo jikan* (Yoe jee-kahn)
Five hours	*Go jikan* (Go jee-kahn)
Six hours	*Roku jikan* (Roe-kuu jee-kahn)
Seven hours	*Nana jikan* (Nah-nah jee-kahn)
Eight hours	*Hachi jikan* (Hah-chee jee-kahn)
Nine hours	*Ku jikan* (Kuu jee-kahn)

Ten hours	*Ju jikan* (juu jee-kahn)
Eleven hours	*Ju-ichi jikan* (juu-ee-chee jee-kahn)
Twelve hours	*Ju-ni jikan* (Juu-nee jee-kahn)

Half	*Han* (Hahn)
One hour and a half	*Ichi jikan han* (Ee-chee jee-kahn hahn)

a.m.	*Gozen* (Go-zen)
Noon	*Sho-go* (Show-go)
p.m.	*Gogo* (Go-go)
Midnight	*Ma-yonaka* (Mah-yoe-nah-kah)

1 o'clock	*Ichi-ji* (Ee-chee-jee)
1 p.m.	*Gogo ichi-ji* (Go-go ee-chee-jee)
1 a.m.	*Gozen ichi-ji* (Go-zen ee-chee-jee)
1:15	*Ichi-ji ju-go-fun sugi* (Ee-chee-jee juu-go-foon sue-ghee)
1:30	*Ichi-ji san jippun sugi* (Ee-chee-jee sahn jeep-poon sue-ghee); also, *ichi-ji han* (ee-chee-jee hahn)

92

1:45	*Ichi-ji yon-ju-go-fun sugi* (Ee-chee-jee yoan-juu-go-foon sue-ghee)
2 o'clock	*Ni-ji* (Nee-jee)
3 o'clock	*San-ji* (Sahn-jee)
10 to 3	*San-ji jippun mae* (Sahn-jee jeep-poon my)
20 to 3	*San-ji ni-jippun mae* (Sahn-jee nee-jeep-poon my)
5 to 4	*Yo-ji go-fun mae* (Yoe-jee go-foon my)

What time is it now?
Ima nan-ji desu ka?
(Ee-mah nahn-jee dess kah?)

Departure	*Shuppatsu* (Shupe-pot-sue)
Go out	*Dekakeru* (Day-kah-kay-rue)
Leave	*Demasu* (Day-mahss)
Get up (morning)	*Okimasu* (Oh-kee-mahss)
Breakfast	*Asahan* (Ah-sah-hahn)
Lunch	*Hiruhan* (He-rue-hahn)
Dinner	*Yuhan* (Yuu-hahn)
Department store	*Depaato* (Day-paah-toe)

What time is it?
Nan-ji desu ka?
(Nahn-jee dess kah?)

What time is your departure?
Shuppatsu wa nan-ji desu ka?
(Shupe-pot-sue wah nahn-jee dess kah?)

What time are we going out?
Nan-ji ni dekakemasu ka?
(Nahn-jee nee day-kah-kay-mahss kah?)

What time are we leaving?
Nan-ji ni demasu ka?
(Nahn-jee nee day-mahss kah?)

I have no more time.
Mo jikan ga nai desu
(Moe jee-kahn gah nie dess)

What time is the appointment?
Yakusoku wa nan-ji desu ka?
(Yahk-soe-kuu wah nahn-jee dess kah?)

What time does the meeting start?
Kaigi wa nan-ji ni hajimarimasu ka?
(Kie-ghee wah nahn-jee nee hah-jee-mah-ree-mahss kah?)

What time shall we get up?
Nan-ji ni okimasho ka?
(Nahn-jee nee oh-kee-mah-show kah?)

What time is the bus leaving?
Basu wa nan-ji ni demasu ka?
(Bah-sue wah nahn-jee nee day-mahss kah?)

We have plenty of time.
Jubun jikan ga arimasu
(Juu-boon jee kahn gah ah-ree-mahss)

What time does breakfast begin?
Asahan wa nan-ji kara desu ka?
(Ah-sah-hahn wah nahn-jee kah-rah dess kah?)

Breakfast begins at 7 o'clock.
Asahan wa shichi ji kara hajimarimasu
(Ah-sah-hahn wah she-chee jee kah-rah hah-jee-mah-ree-mahss)

What time is lunch?
Hiruhan wa nan-ji desu ka?
(He-rue-hahn wah nahn-jee dess kah?)

Lunch will be between 12 and 1 o'clock.
Hiruhan wa ju-ni-ji to ichi-ji no aida desu
(He-rue-han wah juu-nee-jee toe ee-chee-jee no aye-dah dess)

What time is dinner?
Yuhan wa nan-ji desu ka?

(Yuu-hahn wah nahn-jee dess kah?)

Dinner is at 7:30.
Yuhan wa shichi-jee-han desu
(Yuu-hahn wah she-chee-jee hahn dess)

What time do department stores open?
Depaato wa nan-ji ni akimasu ka?
(Day-paah-toe wah nahn-jee nee ah-kee-mahss kah?)

I'll be back in a short time.
Jiki ni kaerimasu
(Jee-kee nee kie-ree-mahss)

Is it time to go?
Dekakeru jikan desu ka?
(Day-kah-kay-rue jee-kahn dess kah?)

I'm sorry, my time is up.
Sumimasen ga, jikan ni narimashita
(Sue-me-mah-sen gah, jee-kahn nee nah-ree-mah-sshtah)

Will this take very much time?
Kore wa jikan ga takusan kakarimasu ka?
(Koe-ray wah jee-kahn gah tock-sahn kah-kah-ree-mahss kah?)

Leisure time	*Hima* (He-mah)
Occasion	*Toki* (Toe-kee)
Early	*Hayai* (Hah-yie)
Late	*Osoi* (Oh-soy)
On time	*Jikan dori* (Jee-kahn doe-ree)

Are you free now?
Ima hima desu ka?
(Ee-mah he-mah dess kah?)

When will you be free?
Itsu hima ni narimasu ka?
(Eet-sue he-mah nee nah-ree-mahss kah?)

At that time, I was in Chicago.
Sono toki watakushi wa Shikago ni imashita
(Soe-no toe-kee wah-tock-she wah She-kah-go nee
ee-mah-sshtah)

I'll go to Kyoto when I have more time.
Motto hima ga aru toki Kyoto e ikimasu
(Moat-toe he-mah gah ah-rue toe-kee K'yoe-toe eh
ee-kee-mahss)

It is late / He/she is late.
Osoi desu
(Oh-soy dess)

It is still early.
Mada hayai desu
(Mah-dah hah-yie dess)

We (they) are going to be late.
Osoku narimasu
(Oh-soe-kuu nah-ree-mahss)

We are on time.
Jikan dori desu
(Jee-kahn dore-ree dess)

23

The Weather

Weather	*Tenki* (Ten-kee)
Weather forecast	*Tenki yoho* (Ten-kee yoe-hoe)
Hot	*Atsui* (Aht-sue-e)
Cold	*Samui* (Sah-muu-e)
Cloudy	*Kumori* (Kuu-mo-ree)
Wind	*Kaze* (Kah-zay)
Rain	*Ame* (Ah-may)
Snow	*Yuki* (Yuu-kee)
Humidity	*Shimerike* (She-may-ree-kay)

Hot and humid	*Mushi atsui* (Muu-she aht-sue-e)
Good weather	*Ii o-tenki* (Ee oh-ten-kee)
Bad weather	*Warui o-tenki* (Wah-rue-e oh-ten-kee)
Rain coat	*Rein koto* (Rain koeh-toe)
Umbrella	*Kasa* (Kah-sah)

It's hot, isn't it?
Atsui desu, ne?
(Aht-sue-ee dess, nay?)

It's cold, isn't it?
Samui desu, ne?
(Sah-muu-ee dess, nay?)

It's cold today, isn't it?
Kyo wa samui desu, ne?
(K'yoe wah sah-muu-ee dess, nay?)

It is raining.
Ame ga futte imasu
(Ah-may gah fute-tay ee-mahss)

It is snowing.
Yuki ga futte imasu
(Yuu-kee gah fute-tay ee-mahss)

How will the weather be tomorrow?
Ashita no o-tenki wa do narimasu ka?
(Ah-ssh-tah no oh-ten-kee wah doh nah-ree-mahss kah?)

Will it rain tonight.
Komban ame ga furimasu ka?
(Kome-bahn ah-may gah fuu-ree-mahss kah?)

It looks like it will rain today, doesn't it!
Kyo wa ame ga furi-so desu, ne!
(K'yoe wah ah-may gah fuu-ree-soh dess, nay!)

It should clear up by this afternoon.
Gogo made ni hareru desho
(Go-go mah-day nee hah-ray-rue day-show)

It's nice weather, isn't it?
Ii o-tenki desu, ne?
(Ee oh-ten-kee dess, nay?)

24

Using Money

Money   *Okane* (Oh-kah-nay)

Yen	*En* (En)
Dollar(s)	*Doru* (Doe-rue)
Exchange rate	*Gaikoku kawase soba* (Guy-koe-kuu kah-wah-say so-bah)
Change	*O-tsuri* (Oh-t'sue-ree)
Small change	*Komakai kane* (Koe-mah-kie kah-nay)
	Kozeni (Koe-zay-nee)
Break a bill	*Komakaku suru* (Koe-mah-kah-kuu sue-rue)
Expensive	*Takai* (Tah-kie)
Cheap	*Yasui* (Yah-sue-ee)
How much	*Ikura* (Ee-kuu-rah)
Budget	*Yosan* (Yoe-sahn)
Tightwad	*Kechinbo* (Kay-cheen-boe)

What is today's exchange rate?
Kyo no gaikoku kawase soba wa nan desu ka?
(K'yoe no guy-koe-kuu kah-wah-say so-bah wah nahn dess kah?)

I want to change $100 into yen.
Hyaku doru wo en ni shitai desu
(H'yah-kuu doe-rue oh en nee she-tie dess)

How much is this in dollars?
Kore wa doru de ikura desu ka?
(Koe-ray wah doe-rue deh ee-kuu-rah dess kah?)

101

Please break this (into coins).
Kore wo komakaku shite kudasai
(Koe-ray oh koe-mah-kah-kuu ssh-tay kuu-dah-sie)

Do you have any yen?
En wo motte imasu ka?
(En oh moat-tay ee-mahss kah?)

This is too expensive.
Kore wa taka sugimasu
(Koe-ray wah tah-kah suu-ghee-mahss)

I forgot my money.
Okane wo wasuremashita
(Oh-kah-nay oh wah-suu-ray-mah-sshtah)

Please loan me five thousand yen.
Go sen en kashite kudasai
(Go sen en kahssh-tay kuu-dah-sie)

25

In a Restaurant

Menu   *Menyu* (Men-yuu)

English menu	*Eibun no menyu* (A-e-boon no men-yuu)
Counter	*Kaunta* (Kah-uun-tah)
Table	*Teburu* (Tay-buu-reu)
Japanese-style room	*Zashiki* (Zah-she-kee)
Grill cooking	*Teppan yaki* (Tep-pahn yah-kee)
Deep-fried foods	*Age mono* (Ah-gay moe-no)
Pot dishes	*Nabe mono* (Nah-bay moe-no)
Broiled dishes	*Yaki mono* (Yah-kee moe-no)
Rice with toppings	*Domburi mono* (Dome-buu-ree moe-no)
Set meal	*Tei shoku* (Tay-show-kuu)
Side dishes	*So zai* (Soe zie)
Boxed food	*O-bento* (Oh-ben-toe)
Salt	*Shio* (She-oh)
Pepper	*Kosho* (Koe-show)
Sugar	*Sato* (Sah-toe)
Soy sauce	*Shoyu* (Show-yuu)
Regular sauce	*Sosu* (Soe-suu)
Bread	*Pan* (Pahn) or *bureddo* (buu-ray-doe)
Coffee	*Kohi* (Koe-he)
Cream	*Kurimu* (Kuu-ree-muu)
Milk	*Miruku* (Me-rue-kuu)
Water	*Mizu* (Me-zuu)

Orange juice	*Orenji jusu* (Oh-rane-jee juu-suu)
Tomato juice	*Tomato jusu* (Toe-mah-toe juu-suu)
Brown (black) tea	*Kocha* (Koe-chah)
Green tea	*Nihon cha* (Nee-hone chah) or *ban cha* (bahn chah)
Coca-Cola	*Koku* (Koe-kuu)
Pepsi-Cola	*Pepushi kora* (Pep-she koe-rah)
Steak	*Suteki* (Suu-tay-kee)
Well-done	*Weru dan* (Way-rue dahn)
Medium	*Mejium* (May-jee-uum)
Rare	*Rea* (Ray-ah)
Chicken	*Chikin* (Chee-keen)
Fish	*Sakana* (Sah-kah-nah)
Dessert	*Dezato* (Day-zah-toe)
Ice cream	*Aisu kurimu* (Aye-sue kuu-ree-muu)
Fruit	*Kudamono* (Kuu-dah-moe-no)
Knife	*Naifu* (Nie-fuu)
Fork	*Hoku* (Hoe-kuu)
Spoon	*Supun* (Sue-poon)
Glass	*Koppu* (Kope-puu)
Napkin	*Napukin* (Nah-puu-keen)
Serving for one	*Ichi-nin mae* (Ee-chee-neen my)

Serving for two	*Ni-nin mae* (Nee-neen my)
Serving for three	*San-nin mae* (Sahn-neen my)
Spicy hot	*Karai* (Kah-rye)
Cold (to touch)	*Tsumetai* (T'sue-may-tie)
Share-seat (table)	*Ai-seki* (Aye-say-kee)
Take out food	*Mochi kaeri* (Moe-chee kie-ree)
Food delivery	*Demae* (Day-my)
Toothpick	*Tsuma yoji* (T'sue-mah yoe-jee)
Chopsticks	*Hashi* (Hah-shee)
Delicious	*Oishii* (Oh-ee-shee)
Tastes bad	*Mazui* (Mah-zuu-ee)

I'm hungry.
Onaka ga suite imasu
(Oh-nah-ka gah sue-ee-tay ee-mahss)

I'm thirsty.
Nodo ga kawakimashita
(No-doe gah kah-wah-kee-mah-sshtah)

An English-language menu, please.
Eibun no menyu wo kudasai
(A-e-boon no men-yuu oh kuu-dah-sie)

I'll take Set Meal "B," please.
"B" no teishoku wo itadakimasu

("B" no tay-show-kuu oh ee-tah-dah-kee-mahss)

Tea with milk, please.
Miruku ti kudasai
(Me-rue-kuu tee kuu-dah-sie)

What kind of fish do you have?
Donna sakana ga arimasu ka
(Doan-nah sah-kah-nah gah ah-ree-mahss kah?)

Please give me / bring me (anything).
(Anything) *kudasai*
([Anything] kuu-dah-sie)

Thank you for the delicious meal.
*Gochiso sama deshita**
(Go-chee-soe sah-mah desh-tah)

*This is a set, institutionalized phrase used to express appreciation when someone pays for your meal or drinks. It is also customary to repeat the expression if you meet the same person a few days later—this time prefacing the phrase with *Sen jitsu wa* (sen jeet-sue wah), meaning "The other day . . . "

In Japanese-style restaurants green tea is served without charge. In Chinese restaurants tea is also generally served as part of the meal. In Western-style restaurants normally only black or brown tea is served (straight, with lemon or milk), and there is a charge. In addition to the commonly served green tea (*Nihon cha* or *bancha*), there is a higher grade of green tea called sencha (*sen-chah*), also:

Roasted barley tea	*Mugi cha* (Muu-ghee chah)
Roasted brown tea	*Hoji cha* (Hoe-jee chah)
Seaweed (tangle) tea	*Kobu cha* (Koe-buu chah)
Oolong Chinese tea	*Uron cha* (Uu-roan chah)
Popped-rice tea	*Genmai cha* (Gane-my chah)

Would you like tea?
Ocha ikaga desu ka?
(Oh-chah ee-kah-gah dess kah?)

26

Paying Bills

Bill	*Kanjo* (Kahn-joe)
Receipt	*Ryoshusho* (Rio-shuu-show)
Cash	*Genkin* (Gen-keen)
Total	*Gokei* (Go-kay)
Mistake	*Machigai* (Mah-chee-guy)
Credit card	*Kurejitto kado* (Kuu-ray-jee-toe kah-doe)

107

The bill, please.
O-kanjo kudasai
(Oh-kahn-joe kuu-dah-sie)

A receipt, please.
Ryoshusho kudasai
(Rio-shuu-show kuu-dah-sie)

Is a credit card OK?
Kurejitto kado de ii desu ka?
(Kuu-ray-jee-toe kah-doe day ee dess kah?)

27

Locating Restrooms

For the short-term visitor in Japan, locating toilet facilities while out on the town is often a pressing need. Toilets available for public use can be found in major office buildings, usually in the first basement and from the second floor on up; in department stores; and in hotels—also usually in the first basement or the first floor, and on the second-floor and/or mezzanine if there are meeting/banquet rooms on those floors.

As in English, there are several Japanese words used to mean toilet.

Washroom	*O-tearai* (Oh-tay-ah-rye) — Polite term, most common.
Toilet	*Toire* (Toe-ee-ray) — Also widely used.
	Toiretto (Toe-ee-rate-toe) — Less common.
	Gofujo (Go-fuu-joe) — Used by women.
	Benjo (Ben-joe) — Old term, now rarely used.
Powder room	*Kesho shitsu* (Kay-show she-t'sue)
Toilet paper	*Toiretto pepa* (Toe-ee-rate-toe pay-pah)
Flush toilet	*Suisen toire* (Sue-e-sen toe-ee-ray)
Uni-sex toilet	*Sen-yo toire* (Sen-yoe toe-ee-ray)
Coed toilet	*Kyodo toire* (K'yoe-doe toe-ee-ray)

Where is the nearest toilet?
Ichiban chikai toire wa doko desu ka?
(Ee-chee-bahn chee-kie toe-ee-ray wah doe-koe dess kah?)

Is there a toilet on this floor?

109

Kono kai ni o-tearai wa arimasu ka?
(Kono kie nee oh-tay-ah-rye wah ah-ree-mahss kah?)

May I use the toilet?
O-tearai wo tsukatte mo ii desu ka?
(Oh-tay-ah-rye oh scot-tay moe ee dess kah?)

28

When Shopping

Shopping mall	*Meiten gai* (May-ee-ten guy)
Shopping arcade	*Akeido* (Ah-kay-ee-doe)
Underground mall	*Chika gai* (Chee-kah guy)
Shopping street	*Shoten gai* (Show-ten guy)
Buy	*Kaimasu* (Kie-mahss)
Want to buy	*Kaitai* (Kie-tie)
Have	*Arimasu* (Ah-ree-mahss)
Do you have?	*Arimasu ka?* (Ah-ree-mahss kah?)

How much?	*Ikura?* (Ee-kuu-rah?)
Expensive	*Takai* (Tah-kie)
More expensive	*Motto takai* (Moat-toe tah-kie)
Cheap	*Yasui* (Yah-sue-ee)
Cheaper	*Motto yasui* (Moat-toe yah-sue-ee)
Large/big	*Okii* (Oh-keee)
Larger	*Motto okii* (Moat-toe oh-keee)
Small/little	*Chiisai* (Chee-sie)
Smaller	*Motto chiisai* (Moat-toe chee-sie)
Gift	*Omiyage* (Oh-me-yah-gay)
Jewelry	*Hoseki* (Hoe-say-kee)
Leather	*Kawa* (Kah-wah)
Books	*Hon* (Hoan)
Book shop	*Hon ya* (Hoan yah)
Look for something	*Sagashimasu* (Sah-gah-she-mahss)
Discount	*Waribiki* (Wah-ree-bee-kee)
Exchange	*Torikae* (Toe-ree-kie)

Written instructions	*Setsumei sho* (Sate-sue-may-ee show)
Thank you gift	*O-rei* (Oh-ray)
Summer gift-giving season	*O-Chugen* (Oh-Chuu-gen)
End-of-year gift-giving season	*O-Seibo* (Oh-Say-ee-boe)

Let me see that, please.
Sore wo misete kudasai
(Soe-ray oh me-say-tay kuu-dah-sie)

May I try it on?
Kite mite mo ii desu ka?
(Kee-tay me-tay moh ee dess kah?)

Are there other colors?
Hokano iro ga arimasu ka?
(Hoe-kah-no ee-roe gah ah-ree-mahss kah?)

I would like to buy a gift.
O-miyage wo kaitai desu
(Oh-me-yah-gay oh kie-tie dess)

Do you have jewelry boxes?
Hoseki bako ga arimasu ka?
(Hoe-say-kee bah-koe gah ah-ree-mahss kah?)

How much is this green box?
Kono gurin no hako wa ikura desu ka?
(Koe-no guu-reen no hah-koe wah ee-kuu-rah dess kah?)

I am looking for a leather purse. Do you have one?
Kawa no saifu wo sagashite imasu. Arimasu ka?
(Kah-wah no sie-fuu oh sah-gah-ssh-tay ee-mahss. Ah-ree-mahss kah?)

How much is that one over there?
Asoko ni aru no wa ikura desu ka?
(Ah-so-ke nee ah-rue no wah ee-kuu-rah dess kah?)

Will you give me a discount?
Waribiki shimasu ka?
(Wah-ree-bee-kee she-mahss kah?)

If I pay cash will you discount (it)?
Genkin haraeba waribiki shimasu ka?
(Gen-keen hah-rye-bah wah-ree-bee-kee she-mahss kah?)

This is too big. Have you a smaller one?
Kore wa oki sugimasu. Motto chiisai no wa arimasu ka?
(Koe-ray wah oh-kee sue-ghee-mahss. Moat-toe chee-sie no wah ah-ree-mahss kah?)

This one is too expensive. Have you a cheaper one?
Kore wa takasugimasu. Motto yasui no wa arimasu ka?
(Koe-ray wah tah-kah-sue-ghee-mahss. Moat-toe yah-
sue-e no wah ah-ree-mahss kah?)

Let's go shopping tomorrow.
Ashita kaimono ni ikimasho
(Ah-ssh-tah kie-moe-no nee ee-kee-mah-show)

I want to go shopping this afternoon.
Kyo gogo ni kaimono ni ikitai desu
(K'yoe go-go nee kie-moe-no nee ee-kee-tie dess)

29

At the Train/Subway Station

Tickets for both subways and commuter trains are
dispensed by vending machines (except in some small
suburban and rural stations), with the fare on the
button to be pushed. There are usually large "fare
maps" on the wall above the vending machines, giving
the fares to each destination on that particular line as
well as on connecting lines.

Unfortunately, most of the destinations are in
Japanese characters (*kanji* / kahn-jee). If you cannot

read or spot your destination, just buy the cheapest ticket on the machine. When you get to your destination, go to the Fare-Adjustment Window adjoining the exit turnstiles and hand the ticket to the attendant. He will tell you how much extra you must pay, and issue you a new ticket to give to the ticket collector at the turnstiles.

Tickets on long-distance trains are generally sold at ticket windows. On "Bullet Trains," first-class tickets, for coaches that are called "Green Cars," are sold at (you guessed it) "Green Windows" (*Midori no Madoguchi* / Me-doe-ree no Mah-doe-guu-chee). Green Cars are *Gurin Sha* (Guu-reen Shah).

Station	*Eki* (A-kee)
Next station	*Tsugi no eki* (T'sue-ghee no A-kee)
Train	*Kisha* (Kee-shah); also, *densha* (den-shah)
Subway	*Chikatetsu* (Chee-kah-tet-sue)
Ticket	*Kippu* (Keep-puu)
Ticket sales place	*Kippu uriba* (Keep-puu uu-ree-bah)
One-way (ticket)	*Kata michi* (Kah-tah me-chee)
Round-trip ticket	*Ohfuku* (Ohh-fuu-kuu)
Boarding Platform	*Homu* (Hoe-muu)

Boarding area	*Noriba* (No-ree-bah)
Entrance	*Iriguchi* (Ee-ree-guu-chee)
Exit	*Deguchi* (Day-guu-chee)
Ticket gate	*Kaisatsu-guchi* (Kie-sot-sue guu-chee)
Central exit	*Chuo-guchi* (Chuu-oh guu-chee)
West exit	*Nishi-guchi* (Nee-she guu-chee)
East exit	*Higashi-guchi* (He-gah-she guu-chee)
North exit	*Kita-guchi* (Kee-tah guu-chee)
South exit	*Minami-guchi* (Me-nah-me guu-chee)
Escalator	*Esukareta* (Ehs-kah-ray-tah)
Express ticket	*Kyuko ken* (Que-koe ken)
Reserved seat ticket	*Shitei-seki ken* (She-tay say-kee ken)
Unreserved seat ticket	*Jiyu-seki ken* (Jee-yuu say-kee ken)
Departure time	*Shuppatsu jikan* (Shupe-pot-sue jee-kahn)
Arrival time	*Tochaku jikan* (Toh-chah-kuu jee-kahn)
Transfer	*Norikae* (No-ree-kie)

Disembark (get off)   *Orimasu* (Oh-ree-mahss)
Board (get on)   *Norimasu* (No-ree-mahss)

What is the platform number for Shinjuku?
Shinjuku yuki no homu wa nan ban desu ka?
(Sheen-juu-kuu yuu-kee no hoe-muu wah nahn bahn dess kah?)

How much is it to Yokohama?
Yokohama made wa ikura desu ka?
(Yoe-koe-hah-mah mah-day wah ee-kuu-rah dess kah?)

Where do I transfer to go to Roppongi?
Roppongi ni iku no ni doko de norikaemasu ka?
(Rope-pong-ghee nee ee-kuu no nee doe-koe day no-ree-kie-mahss kah?)

Excuse me. Is this the train for Tokyo Station?
Sumimasen. Kore wa Tokyo yuki no kisha desu ka?
(Sue-me-mah-sen. Koe-ray wah Tokyo yuu-kee no kee-shah dess kah?)

Is this the right exit for the Keio Plaza Hotel?
Kore wa Keio Puraza Hoteru no deguchi desu ka?
(Koe-ray wah Kay-e-oh Puu-rah-zah Hoe-tay-rue no day-guu-chee dess kah?)

117

Where is the nearest train station?
Ichiban chikai densha no eki wa doko desu ka?
(Ee-chee-bahn chee-kie den-shah no A-kee wah doe-koe dess kah?)

I want to go to Shibuya.
Shibuya ni ikitai desu
(She-buu-yah nee ee-kee-tie dess)

What is the track number?
Nan ban sen desu ka?
(Nahn bahn sen dess kah?)

30

Visiting an Office

Office	*Jimusho* (Jee-muu-show); also *Ofisu* (Oh-fee-sue)
Address	*Jusho* (Juu-show)
Write	*Kakimasu* (Kah-kee-mahss)
Appointment	*Yakusoku* (Yahk-soe-kuu)
Meeting (conference)	*Kaigi* (Kie-ghee)
Floor	*Kai* (Kie)

Hold (conference)	*Kaisai suru* (Kie-sie sue-rue)
Company	*Kaisha* (Kie-shah)
President	*Shacho* (Shah-choe)
Department manager	*Bu cho* (Buu choe)
Section manager	*Ka cho* (Kah choe)
Supervisor	*Kakari cho* (Kah-kah-ree choe)

What is the name of your company?
Kaisha no namae wa nan desu ka?
(Kie-shah no nah-my wah nahn dess kah?)

Where is your office?
Jimusho wa doko desu ka?
(Jee-muu-show wah doe-koe dess kah?)

What is your address?
Jusho wa nan desu ka?
(Juu-show wah nahn dess kah?)

Please write it down.
Kaite kudasai
(Kie-tay kuu-dah-sie)

What is your telephone number?
Denwa bango wa nan desu ka?

(Den-wah bahn-go wah nahn dess kah?)

What floor is your office (on)?
Jimusho wa nan kai desu ka?
(Jee-muu-show wah nahn kie dess kah?)

I will telephone you.
Denwa shimasu
(Den-wah she-mahss)

I have an appointment with Mr. Murata at 10 o'clock.
Murata-san to ju-ji no yakusoku ga arimasu
(Muu-rah-tah-sahn toe juu-jee no yahk-soe-kuu gah ah-ree-mahss)

Where will Mr. Murata's meeting be held?
Murata-san no kaigi wa doko de kaisai shimasu ka?
(Muu-rah-tah-sahn no kie-ghee wah doe-koe day kie-sie she-mahss kah?)

I would like to make an apointment with Mr. Saito.
Saito-san to yakusoku wo shitai no desu
(Sie-toe-sahn toe yahk-soe-kuu oh she-tie no dess)

When will it be convenient for Mr. Saito?
Saito-san no tsugo to shite itsu ga ii desu ka?

(Sie-toe-sahn no t'sue-go toe ssh-tay eet-sue gah ee dess kah?)

Will 2 p.m. tomorrow be all right?
Ashita no gogo no ni-ji de yoroshii desho ka?
(Ah-shh-tah no go-go no nee-jee day yoe-roe-sheee day-show kah?)

I am waiting for Mr. Inouye.
Inoue-san wo matte imasu
(Ee-nou-way-sahn oh maht-tay ee-mahss)

May I use your phone?
Denwa wo tsukatte mo ii desu ka?
(Den-wah oh scot-tay moe ee dess kah?)

31

At the Post Office

Post office	*Yubin kyoku* (Yuu-bean k'yoe-kuu)
Stamp	*Kitte* (Keet-tay)
Envelope	*Fuu-to* (Fuu-toe)
Letter	*Tegami* (Tay-gah-me)

Air letter form	*Ea reta* (A-ah ray-tah)
Airmail	*Kokubin* (Koe-kuu-bean)
Seamail	*Funabin* (Fuu-nah-bean)
Registered mail	*Kakitome* (Kah-kee-toe-may)
Special delivery	*Soku tatsu* (Soe-kuu taht-sue)
Parcel	*Kozutsumi* (Koe-zuut-sue-me)
Mail (send)	*Dashimasu* (Dah-she-mahss)
Weight	*Mekata* (May-kah-tah)
Post box	*Posuto* (Poess-toe)

Where is the nearest post office?
Ichiban chikai yubin kyoku wa doko desu ka?
(Ee-chee-bahn chee-kie yuu-bean k'yoe-kuu wah doe-koe dess kah?)

Do you have any stamps?
Kitte ga arimasu ka?
(Keet-tay gah ah-ree-mahss kah?)

Please mail this.
Kore wo dashite kudasai
(Koe-ray oh dahssh-tay kuu-dah-sie)

Please send this to the U.S. by special delivery.
Kore wo Amerika ni soku tatsu de dashite kudasai
(Koe-ray oh Ah-may-ree-kah nee soe-kuu taht-sue day dahssh-tay kuu-dah-sie)

How much will it cost to send this by seamail?
Kore wa funabin de ikura ni narimasu ka?
(Koe-ray wah fuu-nah-bean day ee-kuu-rah nee nah-ree-mahss-kah?)

Ten air letter forms, please.
Ea reta wo ju-mai kudasai
(A-ah ray-tah oh juu-my kuu-dah-sie)

How many days will it take for this to get to London?
Kore ga Rondon made tsuku no ni nan nichi gurai kakarimasu ka?
(Koe-ray gah Roan-doan mah-day t'sue-kuu no nee nahn nee-chee guu-rye kah-kah-ree-mahss kah?)

What time does the post office open?
Yubin kyoku wa nanji ni akimasu ka?
(Yuu-bean k'yoe-kuu wah nahn-jee nee ah-kee-mahss kah?)

What time does it close?
Nanji ni shimarimasu ka?
(Nahn-jee nee she-ma-ree-mahss kah?)

This is printed matter.
Kore wa insatsu-butsu desu
(Koe-ray wah een-sah-t'sue-boo-t'sue dess)

123

32

Medical Emergencies

Sick	*Byoki* (Be-yoe-kee) Serious enough to see a doctor.
Feel bad	*Guai ga warui* (G'wie gah wah-rue-e)
Catch a cold	*Kaze wo hikimashita* (Kah-zay oh he-kee-mahssh-tah)
Nauseated	*Hakike ga shimasu* (Hah-kee-kay gah she-mahss)
Headache	*Atama ga itai* (Ah-tah-mah gah ee-tie)
Have a fever	*Netsu ga arimasu* (Nay-t'sue gah ah-ree-mahss)
Have diarrhea	*Geri wo shite imasu* (Gay-ree oh ssh-tay ee-mahss)
Be injured	*Kega wo shimashita* (Kay-gah oh she-mahssh-tah)
Toothache	*Ha ga itai* (Hah gah ee-tie)
Stomachache	*Onaka ga itai* (Oh-nah-kah gah ee-tie)
Doctor	*O-isha* (Oh-ee-shah)
Dentist	*Haisha* (Hah-ee-shah)
Hospital	*Byooin* (Bee-yoeh-een)
Clinic	*Kuriniku* (Kuu-ree-nee-kuu)

Examination	*Shinsatsu* (Sheen-sot-sue)
Blood pressure	*Ketsu atsu* (Kay-t'sue ah-t'sue)
Bandage	*Hotai* (Hoe-tie)
Medicine	*Kusuri* (Kuu-sue-ree)
Ambulance	*Kyukyusha* (Que-que-shah)
Be hospitalized	*Nyuuin shimashita* (Knew–een she-mah-ssh-tah)
Operation	*Shujutsu* (Shuu-jute-sue)
Drugstore	*Kusuri-ya* (Kuu-sue-ree-yah)
Insurance	*Hoken* (Hoe-ken)
Health insurance	*Kenko hoken* (Ken-koe hoe-ken)

I am sick. Please call a doctor.
Byooki desu. O-isha wo yonde kudasai
(Bee-yoe-kee dess. Oh-ee-shah oh yoan-day kuu-dah-sie)

Please call an ambulance.
Kyukyusha wo yonde kudasai
(Que-que-shah oh yoan-day kuu-dah-sie)

(Someone) has been hurt in an accident.
Jiko de kega wo shimashita
(Jee-koe day kay-gah oh she-mah-ssh-tah)

Please help (me, us)!
Tasukete kudasai!
(Tahss-kate-tay kuu-dah-sie!)

I caught a cold.
Kaze wo hikimashita
(Kah-zay oh he-kee-mah-ssh-tah)

My head is aching. Do you have any aspirin?
Atama ga sugoku itai desu. Asupurin ga arimasu ka?
(Ah-tah-mah gah sue-go-kuu ee-tie dess. Ah-sue-
puu-reen gah ah-ree-mahss kah?)

33

In the Baths

Bath	*O-furo* (Oh-fuu-roe)
Bathroom	*O-furoba* (Oh-fuu-roe-bah)
Bathrobe	*Basurobu* (Bah-sue-roe-buu)
Take a bath	*O-furo ni hairimasu* (Oh-fuu-roe nee hie-ree-mahss)
Hot water	*O-yu* (Oh-yuu)
Cold water	*Tsumetai mizu* (T'sue-may-tie me-zuu)
Lukewarm water	*Nuruma-yu* (Nuu-rue-mah-yuu)
Shower	*Shawa* (Shah-wah)
Right temperature	*Chodo ii ondo* (Choh-doh-ee-on-doh)

Take a shower	*Shawa wo abimasu* (Shah-wah oh ah-bee-mahss)
Public bath	*Sento* (Sen-toe)
Hotspring spa	*Onsen* (Own-sen)
Mixed-sex bathing	*Kon-yoku* (Kone-yoe-kuu)
Open-air bath	*Roten buro* (Roe-ten buu-roe)

Shall we take a bath together?
Issho ni o-furo ni hairimasho-ka?
(Ees-show nee oh-fuu-roe nee hie-ree-mah-show-ka)

This (water) is too hot.
Kore wa atsu sugimasu
(Koe-ray wah aht-sue sue-ghee-mahss)

Is it all right to put in a little cold water?
Sukoshi tsumetai mizu wo irete mo yoroshii desu ka?
(Sue-koe-she t'sue-may-tie me-zuu oh ee-ray-tay moh yoe-roe-shee dess kah?)

Do you have any soap?
Sekken arimasu ka?
(Sake-ken ah-ree-mahss kah?)

I want to take a shower.
Shawa wo abitai desu
(Shah-wah oh ah-bee-tie dess)

34

Housing

Apartment	*Apaato* (Ah-pah-toe)
Condominium	*Manshon* (Mahn-shone) From "mansion."
Rental home	*Kashi ya* (Kah-she yah)
Rent	*Yachin* (Yah-cheen)
Rental agent	*Fudosan ya* (Fuu-doe-sahn yah)
Deposit (earnest)	*Shiki-kin* (She-kee-keen)
Deposit (guarantee)	*Hosho-kin* (Hoe-show-keen)
Guarantor	*Hosho-nin* (Hoe-show-neen)
Gift money	*Rei-kin* (Ray-keen)
Handling charge	*Te suryo* (Tay sue-rio)
Signature	*Shomeisho* (Show-may-show); also, *Sain* (sine)
Floor mats	*Tatami* (Tah-tah-me)
One tatami area	*Jo* (Joe)
Room/land area unit	*Tsubo* (T'sue-boe) = 2 *Jo*
View	*Miharashi* (Me-hah-rah-she)
Residential area	*Jutaku chi* (Juu-tah-kuu chee)
With bath	*O-furo tsuki* (Oh-fuu-roe t'sue-kee)

In Japan room-size is usually measured in *tatami* (tah-tah-me) mats, the traditional Japanese flooring. One mat is approximately 3-feet by 6-feet, and in this context is called a *jo* (joe)—a *roku-jo* (roe-kuu-joe) room is a six-mat room, or 108 square feet; a *ju-jo* (juu-joe) room is a 10-mat room with 180 square feet of space.

Larger rooms, such as offices, and plots of land are normally measured in *tsubo* (t'sue-bow), which equals two *tatami* mats or two *jo*. A 30 *tsubo* house has 1,080 square feet of space.

I want to rent an apartment.
Apaato wo karitai desu
(Ah-pah-toe oh kah-ree-tie dess)

How much is the monthly rent?
Ik-ka-getsu no yachin wa ikura desu ka?
(Eek-kah-get-sue no yah-cheen wah ee-kuu-rah dess kah?)

Does it have a view?
Miharashi ga arimasu ka?
(Me-hah-rah-she gah ah-ree-mahss kah?)

How many mats is it?
Nan jo desu ka?
(Nahn joe dess kah?)

35

Age

Age	*Toshi* (Toe-she); also *sai* (sie)
Aged person	*Rojin* (Roe-jean)
Old person	*Toshiyori* (Toe-she-yoe-ree)
Young	*Wakai* (wah-kie)

How old are you?
O-toshi wa ikutsu desu ka?
(Oh-toe-she wah ee-kuut-sue dess kah?)
also:
Nan sai desu ka?
(Nahn sie dess kah?)

He is 25 years old.
Anohito wa ni-ju-go sai desu
(Ah-no ssh-toe wah nee-juu-go sie dess)

36

In a Bar

Beer	*Biiru* (Bee-rue)

Black beer	*Kuro biiru* (Kuu-roe bee-rue)
Draught/draft beer	*Nama biiru* (Nah-mah bee-rue)
Light beer	*Raito biiru* (Rye-toe bee-rue)
Cocktail	*Kokuteiru* (Koke-tay-e-rue)
Highball	*Haiboru* (High-boe-rue)
Rice wine	*O-sake* (Oh-sah-kay); also, *Nihon-shu* (Nee-hoan-shuu)
Scotch	*Sukotchi* (Sue-koe-chee)
Whisky	*Uisuki* (Wees-kee)
Whisky with water	*Mizu wari* (Mee-zuu wah-ree)
Bourbon	*Baabon* (Bah-bone)
Wine	*Wain* (Wah-een); also *Budoshu* (Buu-doe-shuu)
Glass of wine	*Gurasu ippai no wain* (Guu-rass eep-pai noh wah-een)
Gin	*Jin* (Jeen)
Vodka	*Uwokka* (Wu-oh-kah)
On-the-rocks	*On-za-rokku* (Own-zah-roke-kuu)
Strong (drinker)	*Tsuyoi* (T'sue-yoe-ee)
Weak (drinker)	*Yowai* (Yoe-wah-ee)
Beer garden	*Biya gaaden* (Bee-yah gahh-den)
Hangover	*Futsuka-yoi* (Fuuts-kah-yoe-e)

Kirin beer, please.
Kirin biiru, kudasai

131

(Kee-reen bee-rue kuu-dah-sie)

Do you have draft beer?
Nama biiru arimasu ka?
(Nah-mah bee-rue ah-ree-mahss kah?)

Another round, please.
O-kawari kudasai
(Oh-kah-wah-ree kuu-dah-sie)

Some tidbits (peanuts, etc.), please.
O-tsumami kudasai
(Oh-t'sue-mah-me kuu-dah-sie)

In some cabarets and clubs, patrons are automatically served a platter of tidbits that may range from tiny sandwiches to mixed peanuts and bean-sized *senbei* (sen-bay) "rice crackers." This "service" is called *chamu* (cha-muu) from "charm," and is aimed at helping to set a convivial mood. There is a charge for the *chamu*.

37

The Telephone

Telephone   *Denwa* (Den-wah)

Public telephone	*Koshu denwa* (Koe-shuu den-wah)
In-house phone	*Oku-nai denwa* (Oh-kuu-nie den-wah)
Domestic phone call	*Kokunai denwa* (Koe-kuu-nie den-wah)
International call	*Kokusai denwa* (Koke-sie den-wah)
Collect call	*Senpo barai* (Sem-poe bah-rye)
Operator	*Kokanshu* (Koe-kahn-shuu)
Telephone number	*Denwa bango* (Den-wah bahn-go)
Extension	*Naisen* (Nie-sen)
Long-distance call	*Cho-kyori denwa* (Choe-k'yoe-ree den-wah)
Call/phone	*Denwa wo kakemasu* (Den-wah oh kah-kay-mahss)
Busy phone	*Denwa wa hanashi-chu* (Den-wah wah hah-nah-sshi-chuu)
Hello	*Moshi-moshi* (Moe-she-moe-she)

Moshi-moshi has two uses. It is the "telephone hello" and is used to attract someone's attention, as when calling out "Excuse me!"

You have a phone call.

Denwa desu
(Den-wah dess)

Just a moment, please.
Sho-sho o-machi kudasai
(Show-show oh-mah-chee kuu-dah-sie)

Who is calling, please?
Dochira sama desho ka?
(Doe-chee-rah sah-mah day-show kah?)

Is Mr. Tanaka in?
Tanaka-san wa irasshaimasu ka?
(Tah-nah-kah-sahn wah ee-rah-shy-mahss kah?)

He is away from his desk.
Seki wo hazushite orimasu
(Say-kee oh hah-zuu-sshtay oh-ree-mahss)

He/she is out now.
Ima gai-shutsu shite imasu
(Ee-mah guy-shute-sue sshtay ee-mahss)

He/she is on another line.
Hokano denwa ni dete imasu
(Hoe-kah-no den-wah nee day-tay ee-mahss)

He/she is in a meeting.

Ima kaigi-chu desu
(Ee-mah kie-ghee-chuu dess)

Shall I have him/her call you?
Denwa wo sasemasho ka?
(Den-wah oh sah-say-mah-show kah?)

Please tell him I called.
Watakushi kara denwa ga atta to otsutae kudasai
(Wah-tock-she kah-rah den-wah ga aht-tah toe
oh't'sue-tie kuu-dah-sie)

38

Visiting a Home

Again there are specific
institutional phrases that are used when visiting
Japanese homes. In their order of use they are as
follows:

Gomen kudasai (Go-men kuu-dah-sie)—This more or
less means "Please excuse me," and is used to
announce one's self at the door or after entering the
foyer, if there is no doorbell. You might say it is the
Western equivalent of knocking on a door or calling

out a very polite "Hello!" In traditional Japanese homes in earlier years, outer gates and doors were generally unlocked during the day, allowing callers to enter the *genkan* (gen-khan) or vestibule before announcing themselves. It is used in the same way today both at private homes and at offices where there is no doorbell or receptionist.

Ojama shimasu (Oh-jah-mah she-mahss)—After you have been invited into a home, and make the first move to enter, it is customary to say *Ojama shimasu,* meaning "I'm am intruding" or "I am bothering you."

Itadakimasu (Ee-tah-dah-kee-mahss)—When served any kind of drink or food, it is customary to say, *Itadakimasu* just before you start drinking or eating. It literally means "receive" and is used almost like a prayer, in the figurative sense of "I receive/accept (this with thanks)."

Gochiso sama deshita (Go-chee-soe sah-mah desh-tah)— *Gochiso* means "treat" or "entertainment"; *sama* is an honorific term for "Miss, Mr. or Mrs." and in this case is used in reference to the host. The colloquial sense is "Thank you very much for the delicious food/drinks."

Ojama shimashita (Oh-jah-mah she-mah-sshtah)—The past tense of "I am intruding," this is used when departing from a home or office. Frequently with *domo* (doe-moe), in this case meaning "very," in front of it.

39

Expressing Thanks

Thanks	*Arigato* (Ah-ree-gah-toe); also, *Domo* (Doe-moe)
Thank you	*Arigato gozaimasu* (Ah-ree-gah-toe go-zie-mahss)
Thank you very much	*Domo arigato gozaimasu* (Doe-moe ah-ree-gah-toe go-zie-mahss) Also the past tenses: *Arigato gozaimashita* (Ah-ree-gah-toe go-zie-mah-ssh-tah) *Domo arigato gozaimashita* (Doe-moe ah-ree-gah-toe go-zie-mah-ssh-tah)
Excuse me/thank you	*Sumimasen* (Sue-me-mah-sen)

The term the Japanese use most often to express

gratitude or thanks is *Sumimasen* (Sue-me-mah-sen) which primarily expresses the concept of an apology— "I'm sorry" or "excuse me"—and only secondarily means "thank you." It is used interchangeably to express both concepts at the same time. It is also the term most frequently used in restaurants and other places of business to attract the attention of waiters and others.

Sumimasen ga (sue-me-mah-sen gah) customarily prefaces any approach to clerks, policemen, officials, etc., when one has a question or a request.

Thanks to you   *Okage sama de* (Oh-kah-gay
                             sah-mah day)

When asked how they are or how they enjoyed a trip or when congratulated on a happy event, Japanese will often preface their thanks with the set phrase *Okage sama de* (Oh-kah-gay sah-mah day), which means "thanks to you"—i.e. *Okage sama de genki desu* (Oh-kah-gay sah-mah day gen-kee dess) or "Thanks to you, I'm fine;" *Okage sama de ii ryoko deshita* (Oh-kah-gay sah-mah day ee rio-koe desh-tah) "Thanks to you it was a good trip."

Thanks to you I had a wonderful evening.
Okage sama de komban wa taihen yukai deshita

(Oh-kah-gay sah-mah day kome-bahn wa tie-hen
yuu-kie desh-tah)

I appreciate your kindness.
Goshinsetsu ni kansha shimasu
(Go-sheen-set-sue nee kahn-shah she-mahss)

Thank you for the meal /drinks.
Gochiso sama deshita*
(Go-chee-so sah-mah desh-tah)

*This institutionalized phrase is said to your host not only
in his/her home but anywhere after eating or drinking at his
or her expense.

Thank you, I've had enough.
Moh kekko desu
(Moh keck-koe dess)

Thank you for your help / assistance.
Arigato, o-sewa sama deshita
(Ah-ree-gah-toe, oh-say-wah sah-mah desh-tah)

I am very thankful to you.
Taihen arigataku omoimasu
(Tie-hen ah-ree-gah-tah-kuu oh-moy-mahss)

Don't mention it / You're welcome.
Doh itashimashite
(Doe ee-tah-she-mah-sshtay)

40

Apologizing

Given their highly sophisticated and deeply en-
trenched system of personal etiquette, which resulted
in extreme sensitivity to verbal and behaviorial slights,
the Japanese are always apologizing out of cultural
force of habit (the key word for expressing thanks—
sumimasen—is also an apology). Most formal acts begin
with an apology; speeches begin with an apology; even
many casual conversations begin with an apology—
almost always the dual-purpose *sumimasen*.

I apologize / Excuse me	*Gomen nasai* (Go-men nah-sie)
Excuse me/I'm sorry	*Sumimasen* (Sue-me-mah-sen)
Forgive me	*Yurushite kudasai* (Yuu-rue-ssh-tay kuu-dah-sie)

In usage, it seems that *gomen nasai,* often expressed in personal situations as *gomen ne!* (go-mane nay!), is the weakest of the above terms. It is most often heard in very casual situations, such as when Americans would say something like "Sorry about that," with little or no emotional content. Mothers say it to their young children. Teenage girls say it to each other. Adults sometimes use it in a teasing manner as well as on more serious occasions.

The strength of the meaning of all these terms is primarily determined by the demeanor and voice of the individual apologizing. Basically, *gomen nasai* and *sumimasen* are interchangeable when used as an apology. When saying "excuse me" to attract someone's attention, it is always *sumimasen*—which sounds like "see-mah-sen" the way it is usually pronounced.

41

Saying Goodbye

Goodbye	*Sayonara* (Sah-yoe-nah-rah) (The literal meaning of *sayonara* is "if it must be so")
Take care	*Ki wo tsukete* (Kee oh skate-tay)

When parting for an extended period of time, or when leaving someone who has been sick or whose health is fragile, other commonly used terms are:

Ogenki de! (Oh-gen-kee day!)

Go-kigen yo! (Go-kee-gen yoe!)

Both of these phrases mean something like: "Go in good health!" or "Take care of yourself!"

When people are seeing a business associate off for a distant or overseas assignment—or when sending newlyweds off on their honeymoon— they will ceremoniously shout:

BANZAI! (BAHN-ZIE!)

three times, each time throwing their hands up in the air. This shout has traditionally been used as a greeting to the Emperor, and as the equivalent of "Charge!" when employed by warriors, soldiers, and other military forces when attacking an enemy. When used today as a farewell, the meaning is something like "Hip! Hip! Hooray!"

PART TWO

42

Pronunciation Guide to
Key Names & Places

A significant part of the communications barrier visitors experience shortly after arriving in Japan—besides not being able to speak or understand Japanese—is the inability to pronounce common Japanese place-names and words. In some cases, this inability includes not being able to pronounce the names of the hotels where they are staying—which is about as basic as you can get.

Learning how to pronounce words is, of course, a lot easier than learning how to "speak" Japanese, but it is still a key part of becoming "fluent" in daily life in the country. By practicing the following pronunciation guides for just half an hour or so you can greatly increase your ability to function effectively in Japan.

43

Country, Islands & Regions

JAPAN / JAPANESE

Japan	*Nihon* (Nee-hoan)
Japanese (person)	*Nihon-jin* (Nee-hoan-jeen)
Japanese (language)	*Nihon-go* (Nee-hoan-go)

THE ISLANDS

Hokkaido	*Hokkaido* (Hoke-kie-doe)
Honshu	*Honshu* (Hoan-shuu)
Shikoku	*Shikoku* (She-koe-kuu)
Kyushu	*Kyushu* (Que-shuu)
Okinawa	*Okinawa* (Oh-kee-nah-wah)
Oshima	*Oshima* (Ohh-she-mah)
Sado shima	*Sado shima* (Sah-doe she-mah)

REGIONS

Tohoku (six prefectures of northern Honshu)
Tohoku (Toe-hoe-kuu)
Kanto (six prefectures around Tokyo)
Kanto (Kahn-toe)

Chubu (nine prefectures in central Honshu)
Chubu (Chuu-buu)
Kinki (seven prefectures around Kyoto–Osaka)
Kinki (Keen-kee)
Chugoku (west side of central Honshu)
Chugoku (Chuu-go-kuu)

There are three other geographically and economically defined regions of Japan, made up of the islands of Hokkaido, Shikoku, and Kyushu.

A district name that one hears constantly is *Kansai (chiho)* (Kahn-sie chee-hoh), which refers to the Osaka–Kobe area.

44

Prefectures & Their Capitals

PREFECTURES	CAPITALS
Aichi (Aye-chee)	*Nagoya* (Nah-go-yah)
Akita (Ah-kee-tah)	*Akita* (Ah-kee-tah)
Aomori (Ah-oh-more-ree)	*Aomori* (Ah-oh-more-ree)

Chiba (Chee-bah)	*Chiba* (Chee-bah)
Ehime (Eh-he-may)	*Matsuyama* (Mot-sue-yah-mah)
Fukui (Fuu-kuu-ee)	*Fukui* (Fuu-kuu-ee)
Fukushima (Fuu-kuu-she-mah)	*Fukushima* (Fuu-kuu-she-mah)
Gifu (Ghee-fuu)	*Gifu* (Ghee-fuu)
Gumma (Gume-mah)	*Maebashi* (My-bah-she)
Hokkaido (Hoke-kie-doe)*	*Sapporo* (Sop-poe-roe)
Hyogo (He-yoe-go)	*Kobe* (Koe-bay)
Ibaraki (Ee-bah-rah-kee)	*Mito* (Me-toe)
Ishikawa (E-she-kah-wah)	*Kanazawa* (Kah-nah-zah-wah)
Iwate (Ee-wah-tay)	*Morioka* (Moe-ree-oh-kah)
Kagawa (Kah-gah-wah)	*Takamatsu* (Tah-kah-mot-sue)
Kagoshima (Kah-go-she-mah)	*Kagoshima* (Kah-go-she-mah)
Kanagawa (Kah-nah-gah-wah)	*Yokohama* (Yoe-koe-hah-mah)
Kochi (Koe-chee)	*Kochi* (Koe-chee)
Kumamoto (Kuu-mah-moe-toe)	*Kumamoto* (Kuu-mah-moe-toe)
Kyoto (K'yoe-toe)*	*Kyoto* (K'yoe-toe)

Mie (Me-eh)
Miyagi (Me-yah-ghee)
Miyazaki (Me-yah-zah-kee)

Nagano (Nah-gah-no)

Nagasaki (Nah-gah-sah-kee)

Nara (Nah-rah)
Niigata (Nee-gah-tah)

Oita (Oh-ee-tah)
Okayama (Oh-kah-yah-mah)

Okinawa (Oh-kee-nah-wah)
Osaka (Oh-sah-kah)*

Saga (Sah-gah)

Saitama (Sie-tah-mah)

Shiga (She-gah)
Shimane (She-mah-nay)

Shizuoka (She-zoo-oh-kah)

Tochigi (Toe-chee-ghee)

Tsu (T'sue)
Sendai (Sen-die)
Miyazaki (Me-yah-zah-kee)

Nagano (Nah-gah-no)

Nagasaki (Nah-gah-sah-kee)

Nara (Nah-rah)
Niigata (Nee-gah-tah)

Oita (Oh-ee-tah)
Okayama (Oh-kah-yah-mah)

Naha (Nah-hah)
Osaka (Oh-sah-kah)

Fukuoka (Fuu-kuu-oh-kah)

Urawa (Uu-rah-wah)

Otsu (Oh-t'sue)
Matsue (Mot-sue-eh)

Shizuoka (She-zoo-oh-kah)

Utsunomiya (Uut-sue-no-me-yah)

149

Tokushima (Toe-kuu-she-mah)

Tokyo (Toe-k'yoe)*
Tottori (Tote-toe-ree)

Toyama (Toe-yah-mah)

Yamagata (Yah-mah-gah-tah)

Yamaguchi (Yah-mah-guu-chee)

Yamanashi (Yah-mah-nah-she)
Wakayama (Wah-kah-yah-mah)

Tokushima (Toe-kuu-she-mah)

Tokyo (Toe-k'yoe)
Tottori (Tote-toe-ree)

Toyama (Toe-yah-mah)

Yamagata (Yah-mah-gah-tah)

Yamaguchi (Yah-mah-guu-chee)
Kofu (Koe-fuu)
Wakayama (Wah-kah-yah-mah)

*Strictly speaking, Tokyo, Osaka, Kyoto, and Hokkaido are not prefectures. Tokyo is a *to* (toe) or "metropolis." Kyoto and Osaka are *fu* (fuu) or "urban areas," and Hokkaido is a *do* (doe) or "district."

45

Other Important City & Area Names

Atami (Ah-tah-me)
Enoshima (Eh-no-sheem-mah)

Fuji-Yoshida (Fuu-jee-Yoe-she-dah)
Gotemba (Go-tem-bah)
Hakodate (Hah-koe-dah-tay)
Hakone (Hah-koe-nay)
Ito (Ee-toe)
Izu (Ee-zoo)
Kamakura (Kah-mah-kuu-rah)
Kawasaki (Kah-wah-sah-kee)
Karuizawa (Kah-rue-ee-zah-wah)
Narita Nah-ree-tah)
Nikko (Neek-koe)
Oshima (Oh-she-mah)
Takarazuka (Tah-kah-rah-zuu-kah)
Toba (Toe-bah)
Yokosuka (Yoe-kose-kah)
Zushi (Zuu-she)

46

Important Names in Tokyo

Akasaka (Ah-kah-sah-kah)—Major international hotels, restaurants, bars, night clubs, and *geisha* inn district. *Akasaka Mitsuke* (Ah-kah-sah-kah Me-t'sue-kay) at the west end of the district is a key subway terminal. Hotels here include Akasaka Prince, New Otani Hotel, and Akasaka Tokyu Hotel.

Aoyama (Ah-oh-yah-mah)—Shops, offices, restaurants, and residential areas.

Asakusa (Ah-sock-sah)—Major transportation terminal, entertainment and shopping area.

Akihabara (Ah-kee-hah-bah-rah)—Noted discount center for electrical appliances and electronic items.

Chiyoda-ku (Chee-yoe-dah kuu)—Tokyo's main westside "downtown" ward. The Imperial Palace is in this ward.

Chuo-ku (Chuu-oh kuu)—Tokyo's main east-side "downtown" ward, where the famous Ginza district is located.

Ginza (Geen-zah)—Tokyo's oldest and probably best-known shopping and entertainment district, which now competes with a dozen or so other districts around the city. In the central area of downtown Tokyo.

Hakozakicho (Hah-koe-zah-kee-choe)—This is the location of the Tokyo City Air Terminal (TCAT), which serves both as the main terminal for limousine buses going to and from the New Tokyo International Airport in Narita and as a check-in facility for many international airlines.

Hamamatsucho (Hah-mah-mot-sue-choe)—This is the

station in south Tokyo where you board the monorail train for Haneda Airport.

Harajuku (Hah-rah-juu-kuu)—A booming young people's district on the west side of Tokyo, noted for its fashion boutiques, restaurants, and Sunday afternoon street-entertainment. Meiji Shrine is located here.

Hibiya (He-bee-yah)—A popular theater and restaurant district adjoining the Imperial Palace grounds on the southeast corner. Also adjoins the Ginza on the east and Shimbashi on the south. A major subway terminal lies beneath its main thoroughfares. The Imperial Hotel is in this area.

Ikebukuro (E-kay-buu-kuu-roe)—An entertainment, shopping, and business center on the northeast side of Tokyo. Several hotels.

Kabuki-cho (Kah-buu-kee-choe)—The primary entertainment area in Shinjuku Ward, about three blocks north of Shinjuku Station. Filled with theaters, restaurants, cabarets, bars, and "soaplands."

Minato-ku (Me-nah-toe kuu)—Tokyo's main south side "downtown" ward, where most embassies and many foreign residential areas are located.

Kanda (Kahn-dah)—An area noted for its book shops and universities. A key train station is on the east side.

Marunouchi (Mah-rue-no-uu-chee)—One of Tokyo's main downtown business centers, adjoining the

Imperial Palace Grounds on the east side. Banks, trading companies, and Tokyo Station are in this section.

Nihonbashi (Nee-hone-bah-she)—Tokyo's original financial center (banks, security companies) and shopping center (major department stores and shops of all kinds).

Otemachi (Oh-tay-mah-chee)—A major financial business and financial center, adjoining the Marunouchi district on the north and the Imperial Palace grounds on the west. A main subway transfer terminal.

Roppongi (Rope-pong-ghee)—One of Tokyo's most popular restaurant, bar, disco, and nightclub areas. On the Hibiya Subway Line.

Shibuya Station and area (She-buu-yah)—A major railway/subway terminal, shopping center, theater, and restaurant district. Several businessmen's hotels. Terminus of the Ginza Subway Line.

Shimbashi (Sheem-bah-she)—Hotels, entertainment, restaurants, and *geisha* inns. Adjoins the Ginza on the south.

Shinagawa (She-nah-gah-wah)—Site of several international hotels some distance south of the downtown area.

Shinjuku Station and area (Sheen-juu-kuu)—A main railway terminal, also a noted entertainment and shopping district and the west-side center for office buildings and international hotels.

Toranomon (Toe-rah-no-moan)—A business and hotel district (Hotel Okura), and the location of the American Embassy.

Ueno Station and area (Way-no)—A main railway and subway terminal, also noted for Ueno Park and its middle-class restaurants, shops, and businessmen's hotels.

Yaesu Guchi (Yie-sue Guu-chee)—East side of Tokyo Station, where the "Bullet Train" platforms are located. In Japanese, these trains are known as *Shin Kan Sen* (Sheen Kahn Sen) or "New Trunk Lines." If you are going to board the trains and are going to the station by taxi, tell the driver to take you to the *Yaesu Guchi* side of Tokyo Station.

Yotsuya (Yoe-t'sue-yah)—Location of Sophia University or Jochi Daigaku; good site for viewing cherry blossoms in April.

Yurakucho Station and area (Yuu-rah-kuu-choe)— Heart of what is usually considered the downtown area of Tokyo, surrounded by the Marunouchi business district, the Ginza entertainment/shopping area, and the Hibiya entertainment and Imperial Hotel district. The station is two short blocks from the southeast corner of the Imperial Palace grounds.

47

Important Names in Kyoto

Aoi Matsuri (Ah-oh-ee Mot-sue-ree), a major festival
Daitoku Ji (Die-toe-kuu Jee), a famous temple
Fushimi-ku (Fuu-she-me coo), Fushimi Ward
Ginkaku Ji (Gheen kah-kuu Jee), the Silver Pavilion
Gion Machi (Ghee-own Mah-chee), Kyoto's famed *Geisha* district
Gion Matsuri (Ghee-own Mot-sue-ree), a major festival
Gojo Dori (Go-joe Doe-ree), a major street
Hachijo Dori (Hah-chee-joe Doe-ree), a major thoroughfare
Heian Jingu (Hay-on Jeen-guu), Heian Shrine
Higashiyama Dori (He-gah-she-yah-mah Doe-ree), a major thoroughfare
Higashiyama-ku (He-gah-she-yah-mah coo), Higashiyama Ward
Jidai Matsuri (Jee-die Mot-sue-ree), a major festival
Kaburen Jo (Kah-buu-rane Joe), a famous theater
Kamigyo-ku (Kah-me-g'yoe coo), Kamigyo Ward
Karasuma Dori (Kah-rah-sue-mah Doe-ree), a popular shopping area
Kawaramachi Dori (Kah-wah-rah-mah-chee Doe-ree), a major thoroughfare

Katsura Rikyu (Kot-sue-rah Ree-que), the famed Katsura Imperial Villa

Kinkaku Ji (Keen-kah-kuu Jee), the famous Temple of the Golden Pavilion

Kita-ku (Kee-tah coo), Kita Ward

Kiyomizu-dera (Kee-yoe-me-zuu day-rah), one of Kyoto's most spectacular temples

Kyoto Gosho (K'yoe-toe Go-show), Kyoto Imperial Palace

Marubutsu (Mah-rue-boot-sue), a department store

Minami-ku (Me-nah-me coo), Minami Ward

Nakagyo-ku (Nah-kah-g'yoe coo), Nakagyo Ward

Nanzen Ji (Nahn-zen Jee), a famous temple

Ni-jo Jo (Nee-joe Joe), probably Kyoto's most famous castle-palace

Nishijin (Nee-she-jeen), a famous silk-weaving area

Oike Dori (Oh-ee-kay Doe-ree), a main street near *Ni Jo* castle

Omiya Dori (Oh-me-hah Doe-ree), "Temple Street"

Sakyo-ku (Sah-k'yoe), Sakyo Ward

Sanjusangendo (Sahn-juu-sahn-gane-doe), a famous temple

Shijo Dori (She-joe Doe-ree), a main street

Shimogyo-ku (She-moe-g'yoe coo), Shimogyo Ward

Shinsen En (Sheen-sen En), a famous Japanese-style garden

Shokoku Ji (Show-koe-kuu Jee), a renowned temple

Shugakuin Rikyu (Shuu-gah-kuu-een Ree-que), Imperial Villa

Ukyo-ku (Uu-k'yoe coo), Ukyo Ward

48

Important Names in Osaka

Akenobashi (Ah-kay-no-bah-she), a place name

Dotombori (Doe-tome-boe-ree), entertainment district

Ebisubashi-suji (A-bee-sue-bah-she-sue-jee), main thoroughfare

Hankyu (Hahn-que), a department store

Honmachi (Hone-mah-chee), a place name

Mido-suji (Me-doe-sue-jee), main thoroughfare

Minami (Me-nah-me), entertainment district

Nakanoshima (Nah-kah-no-she-mah), civic center, on a small island

Namba (Nahm-bah), shopping center, including huge underground mall

Niji-no Machi (Nee-joe-no Mah-chee), "Rainbow Town" underground shopping center

Sakuranomiya (Sah-kuu-rah-no-me-yah), a park

Shinsaibashi (Sheen-sie-bah-she), shopping area

Shinsaibashi Suji (Sheen-sie-bah-she Sue-jee), main thoroughfare

Shin Sekai (Sheen Say-kie), "New World" amusement center

Umeda (Uu-may-dah), a place name

Yotsubashi (Yoat-sue-bah-she), a place name

49

Department Stores

NAME	LOCATION OF MAIN STORE(S)
Daimaru (Die-mah-rue)	Tokyo, Kyoto, and Osaka
Fujii-Daimaru (Fuu-jeee-Die-mah-rue)	Kyoto
Hankyu (Hahn-que)	Sukiyabashi, Tokyo; Umeda, Osaka
Hanshin (Hahn-sheen)	Umeda, Osaka
Isetan (Ee-say-tahn)	Shinjuku, Tokyo
Keio (Kay-e-oh)	Shinjuku, Tokyo

Kintetsu (Keen-tet-sue)	Kyoto
Matsuya (Mah-t'sue-yah)	Ginza, Tokyo
Matsuzakaya (Maht-sue-zah-kah-yah)	Ginza, Tokyo; Kyobashi, Osaka
Mitsukoshi (Me-t'sue-koe-she)	Nihonbashi, Tokyo; Korai-bashi, Osaka
Odakyu (Oh-dah-que)	Shinjuku, Tokyo
Printemps (Puu-ran-tahn)	Ginza, Tokyo
Seibu (Say-buu)	Ikebukuro, Tokyo
Sogo (Soe-go)	Yurakucho, Tokyo; Yokohama; Osaka
Takashimaya (Tah-kah-she-mah-yah)	Nihonbashi, Tokyo; Kyoto; Nanba, Osaka
Tokyu (Toe-que)	Shibuya, Tokyo

50

Major Newspapers

Asahi Shimbun (Ah-sah-he Sheem-boon)

Chunichi Shimbun (Chuu-nee-chee Sheem-boon)
Hokkaido Shimbun (Hoe-kie-doh Sheem-boon)
Mainichi Shimbun (My-nee-chee Sheem-boon)
Nihon Keizai Shimbun (Nee-hoan Kay-e-zie Sheem-boon)
Nikkan Kogyo Shimbun (Neek-kahn Koag-yoe Sheem-
  boon)
Nikkan Spotsu (Neek-kahn Spoe-t'sue)
Nishi Nihon Shimbun (Nee-shee Nee-hoan Sheem-boon)
Sankei Shimbun (Sahn-kay-e Sheem-boon)
Tokyo Shimbun (Toe-k'yoe Sheem-boon)
Yomiuri Shimbun (Yoe-me-uu-ree Sheem-boon)

51

Major Industrial Zones

Chukyo (Chuu-k'yoe)—Aichi and Mie Prefectures
Hanshin (Hahn-sheen)—Osaka and Hyogo Prefecture
Hokuriku (Hoe-kuu-ree-kuu)—Niigata, Toyama, Fukui,
  and Ishikawa Prefectures
Keihin (Kay-e-heen)—Tokyo and Kanagawa Prefecture
Keiyo (Kay-e-yoe)—Chiba Prefecture
Kita-Kyushu (Kee-tah Que-shue)—Fukuoka Prefecture
Seto Uchi (Say-to uu-chee) (Okayama, Hiroshima, and
  Ehime Prefectures)
Tokai (Toe-kie)—Shizuoka Prefecture

52

Other Common Terms

Aka chochin (Ah-kah choe-cheen)—Large, red paper lanterns used by drinking and traditionally styled eating places as symbols of their trade.

Gaijin (Guy-jeen)—This literally means "outside person" and is the common Japanese term for "foreigner." A polite form is *gaijin-no-kata* (guy-jeen-no-kah-tah) or "foreign person."

Jan Ken Pon (Jahn Ken Pone)—The "Paper/Scissors/Stone" hand-game, played on a variety of occasions, for fun as well as points of order.

Jishin (Jee-sheen)—An "earthquake."

Kogen (Koe-gen)—This word is often seen as part of a place-name, particularly those having to do with recreational resorts. It means "heights" and refers to a location in the highlands.

Kawa / Gawa (Kah-wah / Gah-wah)— "River."

Matsuri (Mot-sue-ree)—Another word that is frequently used without translation, it means "festival," of which there are thousands in Japan each year, ranging from tiny neighborhood-shrine celebrations to major national events.

Nagata-cho (Nah-gah-tah-choe)—This is the section in Tokyo where the Diet building and other key government buildings along with the prime minister's official residence are located. It is often used in the sense of "the government."

Noren (No-ren)—These are the short, split indigo blue curtains that are hung over the entrances to Japanese-style eating and drinking places. Shops that serve sushi, noodles, tempura, and the like generally use *noren.* The *noren* are normally hung up when the place opens for business, and taken down when it closes. *Noren* and their emblems have traditionally served as the banner/logo of restaurants and other places of business with long histories.

Shin Kan Sen (Sheen Kahn Sen)—These are the high-speed express trains that foreigners commonly refer to as the "Bullet Trains." The words mean "New Trunk Lines."

Te-miyage and *O-miyage* (Tay-me-yah-gay / Oh-me-yah-gay)—These are the "hand gifts" that Japanese carry when on trips, especially trips abroad, to give to people whom they meet for business or who befriend them. In some business situations, the gifts may be very expensive, but generally they are small tokens.

Zashiki (Zah-she-kee)—Rather freely translated, means a room or rooms in which the floor is made of *tatami* (tah-tah-me) or reed-mats; the traditional Japanese style of flooring. Restaurants serving traditional Japanese-style food often have rooms with *tatami*-mat floors, and ask patrons if they want a *zashiki* or table.

QUICK-GUIDES

Business

GUIDE
TO
JAPAN

*Opening Doors . . .
and Closing Deals!*

Boye De Mente

ISBN 0-8048-1613-1

¥590/$5.95

QUICK-GUIDES

Shopper's
GUIDE
TO ¥
JAPAN

*Getting the Most
for Your Yen!*

Boye De Mente

ISBN 0-8048-1642-5   ¥590/$5.95

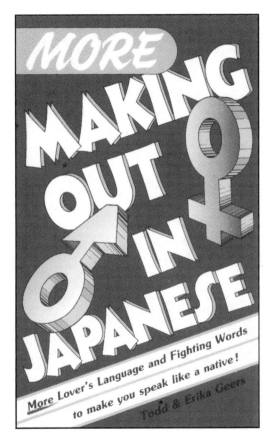

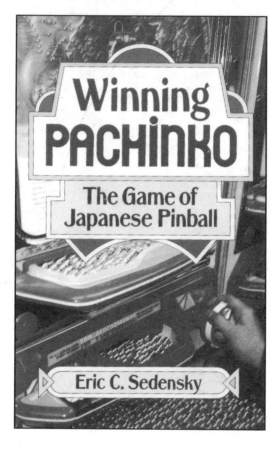

Winning PACHINKO

The Game of Japanese Pinball

Eric C. Sedensky

ISBN 0-8048-1695-6   ¥920/$8.95